During the first decade of my quadriplegia, I earnestly sought healing for my paralyzed limbs and was disappointed that God kept saying no. Over time, I realized that a no answer to my prayers meant a more courageous spirit, an enduring faith, a more buoyant hope of heaven, a deeper engagement in prayer, more compassion for others who hurt, and a rigorous confidence in God's power in weakness. This was a deeper healing that truly satisfied. It is why I am solidly behind the remarkable new book you hold in your hands. In *More Than a Healer,* Pastor Hinn gives thorough and convincing reasons why God does not always heal, as well as the best of reasons for why Christ can always be trusted when there is no miracle. I give this powerful work a solid thumbs-up!

—JONI EARECKSON TADA, Joni and Friends International Disability Center

My friend Costi Hinn has written another vitally important book. He sets our eyes not on what we want Jesus to do for us but on who Jesus really is. As someone who has prayed daily for nearly four years that God would take away my beloved wife's cancer, I can tell you that regardless of what God chooses to do, he has been absolutely faithful to us. My wife, who goes deep in God's Word daily, says, "I wouldn't trade for anything what God has taught me about himself through this cancer." The ultimate healing is in the resurrection, and it awaits all of us who know him. May our hearts overflow with gratitude when he chooses to heal here and now, but may our ultimate hope rest in the blood-bought eternal healing that is his absolute promise. Costi Hinn knows this to be true and is a voice of God speaking hope-giving truth in a world of lies, not only outside the church but sometimes inside.

—RANDY ALCORN, author, *If God Is Good, Happiness,* and *Heaven*

Jesus' healing is far more comprehensive than health, wealth, and prosperity gospel preachers would want you to believe. Our friend Costi's new book can help every Christian understand who Jesus is and how he brought true healing to humanity.

—JINGER AND JEREMY

Counting On; hosts, T

As I read this book, I thought of the tear-streaked faces of so many people I've had conversations with who have been disappointed or disillusioned because God didn't answer their prayers the way they expected him to. And what was the basis of their expectations? They had profound misunderstandings of what God has promised, about how to apply what they read in the Gospels, and what the life of faith is all about. I'm so glad that I can recommend *More Than a Healer* to them in the days to come. What Costi Hinn provides is a corrective for so much of the Christianity lite that is peddled today, which simply doesn't work when the bottom falls out of life. In these pages are winsome wisdom and a gracious invitation into truly experiencing the grace of Jesus in the worst of times.

—NANCY GUTHRIE, author, *Hearing Jesus Speak into Your Sorrow*

The apostle Paul writes to his son in the faith, Timothy, serving as pastor of the church in Ephesus, "Pay close attention to yourself and to your doctrine" (1 Tim. 4:16). Sound doctrine is of paramount importance to the Christian, but sound doctrine must be as much transformational as it is informational. In *More Than a Healer,* Costi Hinn has written a book that is both rich in sound doctrine and immensely practical. Costi combines the skill of an exegete with rubber-hits-the-road practicality. His care with the sacred text as well as his transparency in sharing the trials that he and his wife, Christyne, have recently walked through together make this book a compelling read. Put it at the top of your reading list.

—JUSTIN PETERS, preacher, author, www.justinpeters.org

We live in a broken world full of sin. More than that, we are surrounded by sinners every day. Even more sobering is the reality that we have sin within us—deep within the fabric of our humanity and to the core of our being. Costi Hinn reminds us of our need for Jesus. The truth is, we never outgrow our need for Jesus. Sadly, far too often we are presented with a Jesus who is culturally constructed rather than faithfully expounded from the pages of Scripture. Costi Hinn rightly directs our attention to the Jesus of Scripture, who created the universe and yet is accessible to us on our best of days and during our deepest pain.

—DR. JOSH BUICE, pastor, Pray's Mill Baptist Church; founder and president, G3 Ministries

Costi Hinn's *More Than a Healer* is another excellent appraisal of popular but often damaging misconceptions about Jesus and his work. More than that, this book offers real consolation and real comfort from one who is no stranger to painful trials. This is a soul-stirring work of biblical wisdom and Christ-centered compassion.

—JARED C. WILSON, assistant professor of pastoral ministry, Midwestern Baptist Theological Seminary; author, *The Gospel according to Satan*

Few voices have the potency to speak to the errors of the prosperity gospel and faith-healing movement like Costi Hinn. He's been in that world. He's run in those circles. But he discovered that in Christ we have a far greater treasure and riches than what finances, health, or power can give us. In Christ, we have more than a healer. This book displays the glories of Jesus in dazzling brilliance. In knowing and seeing the real Jesus, our hearts are drawn to prize the Savior for who he is, and not just for what he gives.

—ERIK REED, lead pastor, The Journey Church, Lebanon, TN; president and founder, Knowing Jesus Ministries; author, *Uncommon Trust*

In a time when many in the church are more interested in miracles than in their maker, Costi Hinn makes a simple, bold declaration—Christ alone is sufficient. He is sufficient on the hilltop and in the hospital. He is sufficient in fullness and in famine. Costi hurls these truths at us chapter after chapter, and it's exactly what the church needs.

—DALE PARTRIDGE, president, Reformation Seminary and Relearn.org

My friend Costi has done it again by writing another great book. *More Than a Healer* is timely and needed. Costi urges us to seek the truths about who God is in the midst of trials and tribulations as he explores differing views regarding healing and shows us the need for our only true hope, Jesus Christ. This book is great for individuals, churches, and small groups. Grab a copy for yourself and a friend. You won't regret it, and they will thank you for it.

—SHANE PRUITT, National Next Gen Evangelism Director, North American Mission Board; author, *Nine Common Lies Christians Believe*

MORE THAN A HEALER

COSTI W. HINN

NOT THE JESUS YOU WANT — BUT THE JESUS YOU NEED

ZONDERVAN BOOKS

ZONDERVAN BOOKS

More Than a Healer

Requests for information should be addressed to:
Zondervan, *3900 Sparks Dr. SE, Grand Rapids, Michigan 49546*

Zondervan titles may be purchased in bulk for educational, business, fundraising, or sales promotional use. For information, please email SpecialMarkets@Zondervan.com.

ISBN 978-0-310-36288-3 (audio)

Library of Congress Cataloging-in-Publication Data

Names: Hinn, Costi W. author.
Title: More than a healer : not the Jesus you want, but the Jesus you need / Costi W. Hinn.
Description: Grand Rapids : Zondervan, 2021. | Includes bibliographical references. | Summary: "For a world desperate for healing, author and pastor Costi Hinn presents More Than a Healer, a profound and eloquent work offering biblical answers about God's healing power, wisdom for holding on to faith even in the most painful trials, and help for finding lasting hope in a deep relationship with the Healer himself"—Provided by publisher.
Identifiers: LCCN 2021013466 | ISBN 9780310362869 (trade paperback) | ISBN 9780310362876 (ebook)
Subjects: LCSH: Healing—Religious aspects—Christianity. | Suffering—Religious aspects—Christianity.
Classification: LCC BT732 .H56 2021 | DDC 234/.131—dc23
LC record available at https://lccn.loc.gov/2021013466

Published in association with the literary agency of Wolgemuth & Associates, Inc.

Cover design: Tim Green / Faceout Studio
Interior design: Denise Froehlich

CONTENTS

ACKNOWLEDGMENTS

The concept and title for this book came to mind while I was writing *God, Greed, and the (Prosperity) Gospel*. Now, two years later, it has gone from simply being an idea to becoming another book I believe will point people to Jesus. None of this would have been possible without some key people in my corner.

Erik Wolgemuth is not merely a literary agent to me. He is a friend and colaborer for the gospel. I can't imagine tackling book projects with anyone else.

Carolyn McCready has been instrumental once again as my editor for this project. The synergy we have as a team is a gift from the Lord. She makes *everything* better along the way by asking me tough questions that force me to think deeper as a writer. Beyond the tough questions, she is an encourager and an avid student of the material and has an unparalleled desire for readers to grow closer to Jesus.

My wife, Christyne, was unsurprisingly paramount to this book taking shape. I've become dependent on our routinely deep conversations that go much later into the night than we ever expect. If I doubted her love and care for me (and I don't for a second), I would simply need to remember the amount of time she takes to invest in my life while pouring herself into our four kiddos and caring for others behind the scenes. Eventually people will realize that after Jesus, she is my secret sauce. I don't know anyone who is more detail oriented than my bride, and no one rivals her in her desire to see me glorify God through my preaching and writing.

Last, but never least, I publicly acknowledge that Jesus Christ is the power, the motivation, and the glory of a project like this. This book is about him. What more satisfying journey could one ever take than to disconnect from the distractions of this world and get lost in who he is? I love you with all that I am, Lord Jesus. Thank you.

INTRODUCTION

LORD, WE NEED HEALING!

As I was writing this book, events in the year 2020 unfolded rapidly: the pandemic, cultural upheaval, dramatic battles in the church, the American election. To say that was a wild year is an understatement. It was so unprecedented that the number 2020 came to represent all that is unpredictable in this world. Just when you thought nothing worse could happen, 2020 struck again. It seemed that with every passing month, someone posted something crazy online and said, "2020 is being 2020 again," or, "Just when you thought 2020 was done being 2020."

For our family, pastoral ministry and parenting were challenging in 2020. We welcomed our fourth child (a baby girl named Ruth Joy) into this world during the month of April, shortly after the initial lockdown, while nurses nervously kept us updated on hospital safety protocols and our local government shut down nearly everything in the state. As a pastor, I had to navigate people's different views of the pandemic while praying the church stayed unified. For our church, it went well overall, though we saw the departure of a malcontent or two (or more like twenty). Eventually all sides found common ground, and our leadership team urged people to choose relationships over winning their personal wars. By God's grace, our church exploded spiritually and numerically in the months that followed, and generosity hit all-time highs. We were floored by what God was doing during a time when everything around the world was falling apart. But as I spoke with other pastors and observed the general climate of the body of Christ, it was obvious we were going to face a prolonged time of deep disagreements and conflict. Twenty-twenty seemed like the perfect year for me to be writing about Jesus. Quite honestly, writing this book became a sort of devotional escape for me. As if I were resting in a quiet mountain meadow, my mind and heart were overcome with peace and tranquility as I reflected on who he is. It was healing for my soul even while hell broke loose all around.

Like me, you're probably no stranger to trouble and conflict. You're probably no stranger to the desire for healing as well. Most of us almost constantly seek healing for our lives. Whether it's cancer diagnoses, pain in our bodies, broken marriages, wayward children, splitting churches, mourning communities, or even a divided nation, we are a people in need of healing.

But what if I told you that in our need for healing, we tend to overlook the healer? What if our version of Jesus is so shortsighted that we are missing much of who he is? What if no matter how desperate we are for healing, our need goes far beyond just the Jesus who heals our ailments? What if he offers so much more? Is there a purpose in pain? Is it possible that we have much to learn while we wait on the Lord?

If you're like me, your first response may go a little something like this: "Of course, of course. Jesus is so much more than a healer. He is wonderful, he is love, he is God, he is [insert more Sunday school answers here]. He's a good God. But all of that is exactly why he wants to relieve all my pain. So can we get back to the healing part now?"

Does this response ring true for you? I'll admit, that's the way my mind works at times. And I think if you get brutally honest, maybe yours does too.

In the midst of genuine cries for healing, we tend to miss the healer. We plead for the gift, content to overlook the giver. We don't want to admit it, but could we be seeking God for what he can do, without pausing to relish who he is? Or conversely, in the midst of our suffering, have we declined to ask God for what he has said is possible? Either way, we are missing out on experiencing the "more" of Jesus we desperately need.

Why I Wrote This Book for You

Whether you are rich or poor, thriving or struggling, young or old, healthy or sick, hopeful or hopeless, we all have a lot to learn and relearn about Jesus. These are the reasons I wrote this book:

Reason 1: We Need a Safe Space to Ask Hard Questions about Healing

I used to think I had the topic of divine healing nailed. It was the one subject I thought I knew better than anyone else because it was our family business. For most of my life, until a little more than ten years ago, I was deep in the world of prosperity theology, but once I realized I'd lived and believed a lie that exploited and abused people with false teachings about Jesus, healing, and the gospel, I did what anyone else would do and began to study the truth.[1] Suddenly I encountered *all* of Jesus and the full picture of the good news he preached. Real and lasting hope permeated every area of my life. My thinking changed! No longer did I assume that I could control his healing power or even dare believe that healing could ever be sold for money or special offerings. And more, I began to realize that God works powerfully not just in moments of great miracles but even in the mundane day-to-day lives of those who suffer.

Think about this for just a moment: There are people in this world who right now are not experiencing the healing they desperately desire. Is God still good? Is there hope to be had while they wait for a breakthrough?

Or imagine those living in poverty right now. You could say they need healing financially. At least that's what faith healers might say they need. Can their hope still thrive and their eyes look to heaven for provision? Didn't Jesus show a deep and tender care for the poor? Is he so much more than a healer to them? Can he be more than a healer to you?

Perhaps you're thinking, "These are a lot of questions for just the introduction of a book." You're right. They are. I begin this way because this book is published permission for you to ask any question you'd like. Every page is a safe space for you to challenge me and, if you're willing, to let me challenge you. I want us to explore Jesus together, to think deeply about healing, to look at ourselves in the mirror and pull back the layers of our hearts. Each chapter will end with questions for reflection so we can walk together through every doubt, every hope, every false promise, every unfounded belief, every injustice, and every cry for help you've ever had.

Reason 2: We Need to Get Answers to Hard Questions about Healing

But we're not ending with questions. This book is about finding answers and even going beyond them.

Nearly every week, I interact with people who are confused about healing and Jesus. People from all walks of life are in constant need of healing. Some incessantly chase it, desperate for a breakthrough. They cry out, "God, heal my body!" and, "God, heal my finances, relationships, and brokenness too!" Others feel guilty about asking God for healing, insisting we must be content in our suffering and not make such audacious requests. Still others simultaneously plead and doubt. We indeed are a people in need of healing, but even more so, we're in need of answers.

To complicate matters, revivalists tout healing ministries that promise signs and wonders to all who believe or give their best offerings. Mystics travel the world seeking relief for every ailment under the sun, and millions of desperate souls need only one or two clicks before their smart phones deliver promises of health and wealth from polished televangelists. Everyone is vying for their piece of the healing action. In much of this, Jesus is little more than a product being marketed, and he is known only for one thing—healing! We need answers about healing, but that's not the end of our longing. We are a people who need more of him and less of ourselves. We need to be drawn close to the healer. If we must wait for healing, do we not live for him still? If we are healed, is there not more to know, more to do, and more glorious challenges and victories? I want to show you that there is so much more in store for you in Jesus.

Reason 3: We Need a "Jesus Awakening"

This third reason is the biggest reason. We need a "Jesus awakening." What exactly is that? It's a movement of people who come to know Jesus beyond just what he can do and are reminded of who he is. I want you to discover that Jesus *is* a healer, *and* he is so much more. I want who he is to permeate every area of your life. I want his eyes to be your eyes, his truth to be your truth, his ways to be your ways. This book is about solutions to problems that go beyond mere physical needs. I don't know about you, but I am sick of my selfish inclination toward transactional love. My flesh constantly wants to love God . . . as long as he does what I want and gives me what I believe I need. But what kind of love is that? Do we stand at the altar on our wedding day vowing to our bride or groom, "I promise to love you as long as you do everything I want you to do"? Hardly! But so often we say exactly that to Jesus, not with our words but with our actions—or our *re*actions—when things don't go our way.

We need to wake up and see Jesus for who he truly is and get a fuller sense of what it means to love him no matter what we're going through. Whether we experience healing right now, in the years ahead, or when we reach heaven's gates, Jesus is more than enough for you and me.

This book is your guide to a Jesus awakening.

More of You, Jesus

Can we ever have enough of Jesus? If we think we can, we ought to think again.

John the Baptist said, "He must increase, but I must decrease" (John 3:30 ESV). Paul was so enthralled with Jesus that even in the midst of suffering, persecution, and sacrifice he proclaimed, "To live is Christ, and to die is gain" (Phil. 1:21 ESV). Jesus himself said, "Come to me, all you who are weary and burdened, and I will give you rest. Take my yoke upon you and learn from me, for I am gentle and humble in heart, and you will find rest for your souls. For my yoke is easy and my burden is light" (Matt. 11:28–30). Surely we need more of Jesus.

One of my favorite old-time preachers was no stranger to sickness and challenges in life. Yet he changed the world. His name is Charles Haddon Spurgeon. He was just another human being like any of us, but his perspective during life's tough times was otherworldly. It was Spurgeon who said, "I have learned to kiss the wave that throws me against the Rock of Ages."

Those words are a fitting place to begin. Let's discover more than the Jesus you and I *want*. Let's discover the Jesus we need.

CHAPTER 1

HE IS HEALER

> *When Jesus landed and saw a large crowd, he had compassion on them and healed their sick.*
>
> —MATTHEW 14:14

On August 16, 2018, the clock on the stove read 7:30 p.m. just after we put the kids to bed. It had been a typical—and wildly fun—night in our busy home.

At the time, we had three children ages four, two, and three months old. As with many growing families, our evening moved swiftly through a series of tasks that can sometimes feel like running through an obstacle course. First, there is playtime when I get home from work, then dinnertime, bathtime, cleanup time, family worship (complete with some reading, prayer, singing, and cheesy dance moves), and *then* the kids go down for bed. Of course, there are always a few mishaps along the way when a diaper explodes or controversy ensues over "stolen" toys. Like ducks that smoothly glide across a pond while underneath their feet paddle with frantic effort, my wife and I try to maintain a calm and steady demeanor through much of this, all the while secretly laughing, cherishing, and at times holding back impatience. After all, these days will soon be over, and—with quieter evenings and fewer carpet stains—I'm sure we'll long for one more night of kid-filled chaos. Most nights after the kids go down, we share a few sentiments and have a good laugh over their antics before spending quality time together or doing some other productive task.

But that late summer evening proved to be different.

I had found my way into the kitchen while my wife, Christyne, finished putting Timothy into his crib. As the baby of the family, he was still getting Mommy's special bedtime routine filled with extra cuddles, a favorite song, and a double check on his diaper to make sure he was dry. Beyond that, Christyne was keeping a keen eye on some red spots that had been spreading and had begun to mature into something different from a regular rash on his body. There were now more than a dozen, when just a couple of weeks earlier there were only a few. We had decided to biopsy one of the larger red spots a week prior. Was it just a rash? A skin condition? Maybe he was allergic to something? Speculation would do us no good, so we waited on the results.

After Christyne put Timothy to bed, she logged in to our healthcare account and saw that the results had been shared with us earlier that day. She sent the document to our home printer, picked it up, and brought it to me as I stood in the kitchen.

"Timothy has cancer," she said. Her voice broke as tears filled her eyes.

"Cancer? How do you know? Are you sure?" It felt like someone had sucked every ounce of oxygen out of the room.

She held up the report. "I found the results posted to our account. I don't think they expected us to see them just yet, but I have been checking every day. I don't know why, but I just knew it was something serious. I looked up the technical terms on his report. It's a rare form of cancer."

The tears flowed as I hugged her. We held each other in silence until I said the only thing that kept coming to mind.

"We were never going to get out of this life unscathed, were we?"

She shook her head.

"Now we're going to live what we've been preaching."

There was only one thing we could do. We prayed.

Ironically, for several years we'd been telling others that God is still good, even when things in life are not. We'd made it clear that following Jesus and being a Christian doesn't guarantee health, wealth, and happiness. We'd stood for truth and pushed back against greedy faith healers who exploited people with false promises, and we paid the price for doing so. But compared with facing our child's cancer, every difficulty in our lives leading up this point seemed easy. It felt like all we'd ever stood to lose before was money and family approval. All we'd ever given up was our old life filled with ill-gotten gains in exchange for the greatest treasure of all—Jesus. To be honest, we never felt like we had anything to lose, since we were gaining him.

But now would we lose our little baby boy? It's one thing to suffer or deal with trials personally, but nothing prepares you for the day you hear the C word and your child's name in the same sentence. Christyne and I desperately needed and wanted Jesus to be the healer we knew he was, while not presuming that he owed us healing, as I'd once believed he did.

Questions filled my mind: "How will our families react? What will my family say? What terrible timing—just as we are pushing against abuses by faith healers. Will those faith healers and their followers use this as ammunition to say, 'See! You touched the Lord's anointed, and now look what's happened!'"

I wouldn't have to wait long to get the answers to these questions.

Cancer as a Divine Consequence

We decided to patiently and carefully break the news to certain family members. It was important to us that we have time to pray, process, and then disclose to those outside our immediate circle of friends. One evening, at a larger gathering of family members, I sat down with several to explain what lay ahead and express the certainty of God's comfort in such an uncertain time.

The news about Timothy was swiftly met: "In Jesus' name! He's healed! It's already paid for! No cancer will touch this—"

The remark would have ended with the word house, but the sentence stopped in its tracks. My wife jumped in to hold our ground before I could say anything. It was so outside of her personality that I still remember being both shocked and proud of her.

"We have been praying and will continue to pray for healing," she began firmly. "But we will trust the Lord. And cancer *has* touched this house. We don't want Timothy to die, but no matter what, even if our son dies, God is still good!"

Not a single word of pushback followed.

Several weeks later one extended family member reached

out to me and asked, "Isn't there any part of you that sees the cancer as the result of touching the Lord's anointed?" (He was referring to the idea that speaking out against church leaders—even those who propagate abuses and deception—invites divine consequences.)

My blood boiled at the suggestion that Timothy had been struck by God with cancer. But I replied calmly, "No. I trust that God has a plan and a purpose in all of this, and no matter the outcome, he is good, he is sovereign, and he certainly can heal our son if he chooses to."

"I understand," he responded. And that was that.

While our family may not have said all they were thinking, they'd said enough. If anything, these conversations proved to be a microcosm of a wider way of thinking in our world today. With so many faith healers pounding the airwaves with false promises, and with various degrees of the prosperity gospel finding its way into our churches, countless Christians have at one point or another believed the lie that God is good when things are good and that he is punishing them when things are not. We may even believe that because we are Christians, God owes us a healthy and happy life and must heal us on request. Perhaps no other experience in our lives exposes how we really think about Jesus like sickness does. Everybody struggles with viewing Jesus in transactional ways.

If Timothy's cancer has taught us one thing, it is that God owes us nothing. His grace doesn't guarantee healing, and it doesn't guarantee a perfect life. We've also been reminded that Jesus' healing ministry gets some really bad press these days.

For the rest of this chapter, I promise to help you discover (or rediscover) truths that will silence the noise you've heard—and the lies you've been told—about Jesus and his healing ministry. After that I want to offer you some practical questions for reflection, which you can use to search your heart and seek comfort from Christ.

The Healing Debate

Plenty of opinions about divine healing muddy the waters of truth and steal your joyful assurance that God cares about your pain. With lots of nuance in between, two extremes tend to make the most noise in the church today.

- *Extreme 1: It's always God's will to heal right now.* This view is held by faith healing enthusiasts who teach that something is wrong with your faith if you're sick. They teach that your lack of faith is the problem or that you aren't giving enough money to activate the blessing of divine healing on your life. Still others claim that your healing is already completed and paid for by Christ's death on the cross. You simply need to start speaking it into reality by saying, "I am healed!" That thinking is where we get the phrase "name it and claim it." Last, as in our family's case, some people believe that you would have been healed if you hadn't spoken against faith healers. I used to believe and propagate these hurtful lies.
- *Extreme 2: Jesus doesn't heal at all.* This view, obviously, is held by atheists and others who don't acknowledge the existence of God, but it is also held by Christians who believe that Jesus doesn't heal anymore. The technical term for this belief is "full cessationism," which teaches

that God does not do any miracles today. Our supernatural God isn't supernatural these days. This view is as foolish as it sounds. God is a supernatural God and most certainly still heals and works miracles today. Does that mean every miraculous claim is legitimate? No. But we should not assume a "hold on for dear life until Jesus comes back" mentality. This view crushes the hearts of the sick and the hurting, because it misses the truth about divine healing. If you believe in God, you must believe that he is supernatural, because he is!

Both of these extreme views fall terribly short of what God has made clear in the Bible. Worst of all, they put words in Jesus' mouth. Jesus can and does heal today. But that doesn't mean he is obligated to do so. Still, do not ever give ear to someone who claims that God does not heal today. One of his names in the Bible is *Yahweh-rophe* ("the Lord, your healer"), which is used in Exodus 15:26 (ESV) to identify God as one who heals the sick.

The God of the Improbable

I have a dear friend who is exactly the kind of friend you'd like to have. His name is Daniel, and aside from being a Raiders fan (NFL football), there is nothing you wouldn't like about him. He is kind, prayerful, loving, generous, loyal, and dependable. To this day, whenever we talk, it's as though we were together just yesterday, even though he now lives in Colorado and I am in Arizona. But before time apart and physical distance marked our friendship, we were together in Southern California. When my wife and I first came to the church in Orange County, we were in a small group with Daniel and his wife, Daniela (yes, their names are real and adorably close). We loved them dearly and still do. Which is why it struck our hearts so deeply when Daniel was diagnosed with Hodgkin's lymphoma. But his diagnosis wasn't the final word. I'll let Daniel take it from here.

> My cancer story starts well before my condition was diagnosed. In the fall of 2012, I had landed my dream job at Open Doors USA—a nonprofit that helps persecuted Christians around the world. Almost immediately after I was hired, my wife, Daniela, and I traveled to Colombia to check out a project, and while we were there, we fell in love with the church. We wanted to go back to visit as soon as possible.
>
> However, a couple of months before our second trip, I began to experience constant headaches and physical exhaustion. After going to the doctor and being told that it was stress, I waited a few more weeks before I returned to the doctor's office to press the issue. This time, I was given a blood test and told that I would get my results in a few weeks. After not hearing back from my doctor, and because I was shortly going to Colombia, I decided to call so I could get the news that all was well. The doctor, however, did *not* tell me that all was well. Rather he told me that I was anemic and would need a colonoscopy to figure out why.
>
> When we reached Colombia in February 2013, the staff that remembered me from our previous visit made comments about how I did not look well—funny how others could tell but I couldn't. What I did notice, though, was how exhausted I felt and how I had to miss out on a few activities because of my fatigue.

Upon our return to the United States, I began my follow-up appointments. After my colonoscopy, the GI doctor, who listened to my wife's concerns about the swollen lymph nodes on my neck, immediately ordered a biopsy. When my family heard about my need for a biopsy, my brother and his family drove from Colorado to California to be there for us—though I was still convinced it was nothing—and we filled up that biopsy waiting room like it was a family reunion. The results, though, were far from joyous.

I can still remember that day vividly. I remember the gray sky, the look on my wife's face, and the absolute breakdown she had when the doctor told us that it was cancer—Hodgkin's lymphoma, to be exact.

Immediately the cancer treatment preparations began. Our doctor recommended that we freeze my sperm to help ensure that we could have kids in the future. I had never considered that chemo would affect my fertility. What nobody knew is that Daniela had already been told by her doctor that she was infertile. Would we have liked kids of our own? Sure. But to be honest, we knew that adoption or opportunities like living in Colombia would be possible if we didn't have kids. All in all, we didn't see the inability to have our own children as a negative, but more as a fact. We simply trusted God's will. If God wanted us to have kids, he'd cause us to have kids. But for now, the doctors said it wasn't going to happen.

My first session of chemotherapy started on May 2, and I was scheduled to have a chemo session every two weeks until October 3. I remember in the midst of chemo actually being excited for the opportunity to go through it. It was as if this was my time to show the world what I really believed about

> God, to be a spectacle for the world to see so that I could honor God. I can't quite explain what this was like, but I believe that the empowering of the Holy Spirit gave me joy and excitement to have been selected for this trial. I was also deeply encouraged because we were clearly not alone. Our church family, as well as our blood family, supported us in whatever way we needed—they brought us meals, drove and accompanied me to my chemo sessions, prayed with us and for us, and the list goes on. We even received gifts from people we'd never met before and still haven't met to this day! To say that cancer wasn't a burden for me would be an accurate statement, but for Daniela it was devastating. We often say our cancer story was harder on her than on me.

So how did Daniel's story end? By December 14, 2014, doctors declared he was cancer free. The treatments had worked. But that wasn't the supernatural part. Along with Daniel's being cancer free, Daniela was pregnant. The impossible thing that doctors said would never happen had happened. *That* was nothing short of God's power and grace on their lives. Jesus, the Great Physician, saw fit to use doctors and chemo to heal one issue and to leave doctors speechless concerning another. How did it happen? Did God perform a divine surgery? Were the doctors wrong? Did Daniela's body heal itself? These questions are valid and, regardless of the speculation, the reality remains the same: something happened that was out of the ordinary. Refreshingly, there was no fanfare or faith healing spectacle.

My purpose in sharing Daniel and Daniela's story is not to give you false hope or to be sensationalistic but to help us stay balanced and humble in our approach to the subject of healing.

Their story is an encouraging reminder to me that God can work in improbable ways that go beyond our comprehension. He works powerfully through doctors, he works powerfully without doctors, he can overcome any obstacle, and he can do what human opinions say cannot be done.

My guess is that you know people who've experienced similar breakthroughs. But does that mean it's always God's will to heal right now? What about people who are sick for years? If Jesus paid for sickness on the cross, then why don't we instantly get healed when we are saved by faith in him? If God is always good, isn't healing guaranteed?

He most certainly is good. And he is the God of guarantees, the God who keeps his promises. But his guarantees for healing don't necessarily mean we'll like the timing.

In the next two sections of this chapter, I want to address two big questions about sickness and healing. The first question is, why do people get sick? And the second is, is it always God's will to heal right now?

First Big Question: Why Do People Get Sick?

This is one of the most pressing questions when it comes to healing, and it must be answered by using the Scriptures. Opinions and abuses abound, so the only way to address this question is to cement ourselves in the truth of God's unchanging Word.

I've seen it time and time again, and I'm sure you have too. A world-renowned faith healer hits the news after promising to heal people, but only if they pay up first. Some even go so far as to say that God is going to pour down judgment on people if they don't give a certain amount of money. These "healers" appear to have all the answers for sickness. Years ago I sat through many services in which a faith healer explained to people why they were sick. Some people were told that they weren't giving enough money, others apparently were not forgiving people, and others had been spending time with negative people. Not only that but some were said to be sick because they just didn't have enough faith. This sort of guesswork breaks hearts, leads lives astray, and spiritually abuses desperate people.

Thankfully, the Bible breaks such deceptive bondage. If you've ever been confused about why people get sick or you know someone who needs answers, the following truths will be a soothing balm to a weary soul.

Truth 1: Sickness and Death Entered the World through Original Sin

On the sixth day of creation, the Bible tells us, "God saw all that he had made, and it was very good" (Gen. 1:31). Notice it doesn't say "some of what he had made was very good." It says *all*. There was no sin in the world, sickness did not exist, and Adam and Eve were set to enjoy a flawless life complete with a perfect relationship with God.

Instead they were deceived by the serpent and disobeyed the one command God had given them to follow. This is what is called "original sin," because it was the first sin the world had ever known, and it resulted in a fractured relationship between God and his creation (Gen. 3:1–19).

Because of sin, fear and shame came upon humanity (vv. 7, 10), marital relationships experience conflict (v. 16), women experience pain in childbirth (v. 16), and work became incredibly difficult (vv. 17–18). Worst of all, death entered the scene and humankind would return to dust (v. 19). Sickness and death are the result of sin and the fallen world we live in. Because of sin, we need a savior. And while true Christianity looks forward to that day when Jesus will return and restore all things, until then we must realize that sickness and death are part of this temporary life. Thankfully, eternal life knows nothing of such things.

Truth 2: Sickness and Death Can Strike Us because of Our Own Sin

Using the Bible again, let's face the truth that sickness and death can strike us through our sin. In 1 Corinthians 11:27–30, Paul says that taking Communion in an unworthy manner is the reason why some people are weak, sick, or "asleep" (a biblical expression for death). This is a statement made directly to the New Testament church. Taking Communion unworthily includes not taking it seriously, not examining oneself as Paul instructs (v. 28), having impure motives, having unconfessed deliberate sin, and being embittered and unforgiving toward others (the very opposite of what Communion represents, since we've been forgiven).

Another reason why sickness and death can result from sin is based on the law of consequences, the idea that "a man reaps what he sows" (Gal. 6:7). If you do drugs, drink and drive, act foolishly and belligerently, take poor care of your body, engage in rampant and casual sex outside of marriage, might you not at some point experience sickness or death (often prematurely)? Sin often does lead to these things. Therefore when we examine our lives and the reason for some unfortunate experiences, we must be sure to know the difference between what is self-inflicted sickness or death and what is a genuine trial or tribulation that we did nothing to cause (James 1:2–4; Rom. 5:3–5). Should you find yourself convicted by the Holy Spirit concerning sin that is causing your sickness, take hold of Jesus' beautiful grace. Confess your sin and he will forgive you and cleanse you (1 John 1:9), and then you should go to the elders of your church and ask them to pray for you, as well as confess your sin and be honest with them about your situation (James 5:13–16). God's Word says that in this context, "the prayer of a righteous person has great power" (v. 16 ESV).

Truth 3: Sickness and Death Are Not Always the Result of Our Sin

It's impossible to diagnose the reason for everyone's sickness, but we could certainly say that most if not all of God-loving, sin-confessing, Jesus-believing Christians who are sick fall into this third category. If original sin isn't the only culprit, then a certain situation in Jesus' ministry can shed some light on why some are sick. The gospel of John recounts the story.

> As [Jesus] went along, he saw a man blind from birth. His disciples asked him, "Rabbi, who sinned, this man or his parents, that he was born blind?"
>
> "Neither this man nor his parents sinned," said Jesus, "but this happened so that the works of God might be displayed in him. As long as it is day, we must do the works of him who sent me. Night is coming, when no one can work. While I am in the world, I am the light of the world."
>
> After saying this, he spit on the ground, made some mud with the saliva, and put it on the man's eyes. "Go," he told

> him, "wash in the Pool of Siloam" (this word means "Sent"). So the man went and washed, and came home seeing.
>
> —JOHN 9:1-7

This story is an incredible lesson to all of us that what we might think is the reason for sickness isn't always the reason. Our finite human wisdom gets us only so far. Jesus makes it clear that God's purposes and ways are far above our pay grade and that we do not control his plan and schedule. *Sometimes* God allows certain things or determines how long a circumstance will last so he can showcase his infinite power and wisdom and reveal more of himself to us. We wouldn't praise him for his mercy if we weren't aware of his wrath. We wouldn't appreciate his love for sinners if we didn't realize his hatred of sin. In the same way, we couldn't begin to glorify him for his healing hand if we didn't experience (or see) sickness.

This leads to the fourth and final truth in this section. Buckle up. You may not like it—at first.

Truth 4: God Can Use Sickness and Death for His Glory and the Good of Others

Just because God is not the cruel originator of sickness does not mean he can't use it. He is God, and nothing is outside of his scope of authority. Sin may have brought sickness into this world, but God gets the final word.

You might be thinking I've lost my mind to think that God could somehow bring something good out of sickness, but before you give up on me, let's dig deeper. For starters, nowhere in Scripture do we find God to be a cosmic abuser who gets joy out of striking his children with sickness in the name of growth and glory. That is not what this truth means. However, the Bible does give us a hopeful perspective about sickness, suffering, trials, and even death that helps us sift through the broken pieces these often leave at our feet.

God is strong enough, wise enough, and powerful enough to bring purpose out of our pain, even if he doesn't take *us* out of the pain right away.

You and I experience this more often than we realize. Whenever someone we know dies, it can lead either to bitterness toward God or to our appreciation of the gift of relationships and the life we've been given. Of course, the grieving process may be arduous, but he never leaves us there alone. Furthermore, our grief often matures us to a place where we are able to encourage and support others when they go through what we have gone through.

Romans 8:28 says, "We know that in all things God works for the good of those who love him, who have been called according to his purpose." This passage is often thrown around as a broad promise that everything is going to turn out the way we want it to. But God wants us to understand important truths from it before we jump to conclusions. First, "all things" means the good, the bad, and the ugly. I think sometimes we miss that fact and jump right to thinking, "God is going to make everything perfect." God doesn't promise that nothing bad will happen to us, but he does promise that all those things "work together for good" (ESV). And remember, whose definition of good are we talking about here? His! Which means that however God chooses to define good is what is ultimately best, even if we don't always understand it at the time. "All things" includes a cancer diagnosis, and "good" could mean that you are going to pray more than ever before and be closer to Jesus than you've ever been. "All things" includes losing a loved one, and "good" could be the opportunity you have to share the hope and saving love of Jesus Christ at the funeral. "All things" includes the loss of a child, and "good" could mean the beginning of a ministry to parents who are grieving the loss of children.

My friend Nancy Guthrie is the author of numerous resources on grief, suffering, and God's character. She recently wrote *God Does His Best Work with Empty* and has experienced exactly what this fourth truth is all about.

She and her husband, David, endured two "all things," one with a doctor's report stating that their newborn daughter Hope had a rare metabolic disorder and would not live past her first birthday, and the second with their newborn son Gabriel, who lived 183 days. As for God's bringing about "good" through all of this? He chose to bring purpose to their pain by using Nancy and David to speak to hundreds of thousands of grieving parents who need hope in the midst of their own tragedies and loss. Does anyone ever pray to lose a daughter and a son in order to gain a life-changing ministry? Never. But Nancy's perspective on why she wrote her first book about their family's story shows us what God can do in the midst of—even through—our deepest pain: "I wrote the book not to exploit our babies' lives but to use our experience, like Job, to address the question of suffering: 'To what purpose? What is it God wants to do in you and through you that could possibly cost you this much?'"[2]

The ability to surrender our lives to Jesus is the mark of spiritual maturity. The right perspective on who Jesus is will cause us to raise our hands in surrender, saying, "Jesus, this situation hurts and I don't know all the answers, but I know that you can take pain and turn it into purpose. So have your way. Thy will be done. You are the potter; I am the clay. Turn this situation around so that it brings blessing to others and glory to your name. Whatever that looks like is fine with me."

We need to pray for the greatest good, a practice endorsed by legendary Harvard graduate, theologian, and pastor James Montgomery Boice. On Sunday, May 7, 2000, in Philadelphia, Pennsylvania, Boice took to the pulpit to address his congregation. Countless members of Tenth Presbyterian Church had been asking how they might serve and pray for him during his battle with terminal cancer. What Boice said that Sunday captures the perspective which can come only from spending time with Jesus and cultivating a life that emulates the humility and surrender of the Healer himself. He explained,

> A number of you have asked what you can do, and it strikes me that what you can do, you are doing. This is a good congregation, and you do the right things. You are praying, certainly, and I've been assured of that by many people. And I know of many meetings that have been going on. A relevant question, I guess, when you pray is, pray for what? Should you pray for a miracle? Well, you're free to do that, of course. My general impression is that the God who is able to do miracles—and he certainly can—is also able to keep you from getting the problem in the first place. So although miracles do happen, they're rare by definition. A miracle has to be an unusual thing. I think it's far more profitable to pray for wisdom for the doctors. Doctors have a great deal of experience, of course, in their expertise, but they're not omniscient—they do make mistakes—and then also for the effectiveness of the treatment. Sometimes it does very well and sometimes not so well, and that's certainly a legitimate thing

> to pray for. Above all, I would say pray for the glory of God. If you think of God glorifying himself in history and you say, where in all of history has God most glorified himself? He did it at the cross of Jesus Christ, and it wasn't by delivering Jesus from the cross, though he could have. Jesus said, "Don't you think I could call down from my Father ten legions of angels for my defense?" But he didn't do that. And yet that's where God is most glorified.[3]

These four biblical truths are helpful, but they are also extremely humbling. In the end, we won't always have the answers, but we can certainly have the Answer. Jesus can and will cause anything and everything to work out for good. We must remember what that means.

Now that we understand a bit better why people get sick, let's turn to the second big question about sickness and healing.

Second Big Question: Is It Always God's Will to Heal Right Now?

On a family camping trip in California not long ago, I met a faith healer in the most unlikely of ways. Our first night on the campground, a man walked up to my campsite out of the blue, introduced himself, sat down, and spent the better half of two hours telling me about his divine-healing ministry. Though made aware of it, he did not offer to heal my wife's asthma, but he did give me two copies of his book about the power of words and offered some insights on how to heal every sick person I knew. Unfortunately, he could talk about the theories but couldn't practice what he preached. As the night wore on, I mentioned that

I was a pastor—which only further excited him. He eventually offered me four hundred of his books for our church (discounted, of course) to help our people take hold of healing power. Not long after that, I revealed my knowing a thing or two about faith healing, and faith *healers*. After a firm yet loving encouragement regarding his wayward teachings, we said goodnight. He did not come back, though I certainly would have welcomed a spirited follow-up discussion.

A perusal of certain Christian television networks tells a similar story. There you'll find healing televangelists claiming that it's always God's will to heal you right now—if the price is right.

So is it always God's will to heal right now? Let's look at four simple truths from the Bible that will liberate you from the hurtful burden of believing something is wrong with you if you aren't receiving your healing just yet.

Truth 1: God Doesn't Heal Everyone All the Time

The most important starting point for any discussion on healing is the affirmation that though God *does* heal, he doesn't heal everyone all the time. The Bible gives irrefutable evidence to support this. During Jesus' earthly healing ministry, he didn't always heal everyone. Jesus healed just one man out of a multitude of sick people at the Pool of Bethesda (John 5:3–8) and didn't heal people in his hometown of Nazareth (Matt. 13:58). After a healing spree in the district of Galilee, Jesus plainly decided to move on, even though desperately sick and hurting people were looking for him. His reason was simple: "Let us go somewhere else—to the nearby villages—so I can preach there also. That is why I have come" (Mark 1:38). Christ didn't come to earth merely to hold a healing crusade; he came to bring salvation. More on that in chapter 3, "He Is Savior."

That God doesn't heal everyone all the time is clear from the life of Jesus. It is also clear from the writings of the most prolific apostle, who authored thirteen New Testament books. Paul could perform miracles, yet he told Timothy to take wine for his stomach (1 Tim. 5:23). Why didn't the apostle exercise his gift of healing? Paul also left one of his faithful ministry teammates, Trophimus, sick at Miletus (2 Tim. 4:20). Why didn't he heal him and bring him along?

Clearly, God heals as he wills, and his healing power is not a formula that anyone can master.

Truth 2: God Doesn't Heal Based Solely on One's Faith

Can you believe your way into getting healed? This view on faith healing was first popularized in the early twentieth century by faith healing evangelists, though I am sure it happened before radio and television took it into the mainstream. These individuals made a lot of money off of people by making them repeat customers to their healing crusades. If someone didn't get healed, the faith healer blamed the sick person and told them to come back with more faith—and usually an offering. (We'll deal with that one next.) Fortunately, the Bible clears the air on this abusive teaching.

When Jesus healed the cripple at Bethesda, the man didn't have a clue who Jesus was, let alone have enough faith (John 5:13). In Luke 5:17–26, Jesus did heal based on faith: he healed a man's soul through salvation. And when the Pharisees questioned his authority to forgive the lame man's sins, Jesus healed the man physically to prove it. Other times, Jesus was moved by people's faith, but this doesn't mean his healing touch was bound to whether they had enough faith.

When the woman with the bleeding issue crawled through the crowd just to touch the hem of Christ's robe, he felt power leave him (Luke 8:46). Jesus, moved by her faith, healed her, but he also told her of the healing that had taken place in her soul, saying, "Daughter, your faith has healed you. Go in peace" (v. 48). Jesus called her "daughter" because he offered the greatest healing of all; she was now part of the family of God.

So can the healing power of Christ be coerced by faith? No. Jesus is the Great Physician who focuses on healing the soul, not merely the body.

Truth 3: God Doesn't Perform Healing for a Price

Simon the Sorcerer tried to buy it (Acts 8:9–25), fortune-tellers and witch doctors will sell it, and faith healers will tell you to sow your biggest seed to get it. As it has been throughout history, many people are convinced that healings, like houses, are for sale. When a beggar asked for a blessing in his cup, the apostle Peter offered him something better—and gave it to him for free (Acts 3:6). This truth is pure, sweet, healing truth for your weary and burdened mind. You don't need to go broke to get healed. If Jesus can't be forced to heal by the right amount of faith, then it's unthinkable that the Alpha and Omega can be bribed with money into healing you. No apostle, no New Testament writer, and not even Jesus himself ever told someone to give a financial seed of faith for a healing, a breakthrough, or protection from sickness. It is not God's will that you give money to be healed. Instead it's God's will that you be liberated from such hurtful lies.

Truth 4: God Will Heal All Believers in Heaven

The atonement bought and paid for everything you and I could never afford. Christ died and paid the penalty of sin, whose consequences are sickness, tears, fears, the wrath of God, and an eternal separation from God in hell. While all of this (and more) is provided for in the atonement, many of the blessings we'll experience won't be fully realized until heaven. While we have assurance of salvation through faith in Jesus Christ here on earth, we don't live eternally until after we die (John 3:16). Similarly, although we know this old decaying body will be replaced by a glorified one (1 Cor. 15:50–53), it doesn't matter how much you go the gym; you won't have your ultimate body until you get to heaven. Finally, Christ said he is going to prepare a place for his disciples (John 14:2–3), and that means us too. Yet many of us would hardly call our current home a heavenly mansion. Yes, all of the benefits of the atonement were paid for by Christ, but heaven is where we'll eternally enjoy them in the fullest sense.

One day the trumpet will sound, the dead in Christ shall rise, death will be no more, he'll wipe away every tear, cancer won't exist, wheelchairs will be good only for scrap metal, blindness will be overcome by marvelous light, and the glorious blessings of the atonement will be realized once and for all in eternity.

Some will experience the sovereign healing hand of God in this life. And others will suffer and not be healed until heaven. In every circumstance, let these truths from the Word of God bring comfort to your soul and to your body: Your years of suffering and uncertainty are but a vapor here on earth. Your eternity of perfect joy will never end.

Does God still heal today? As the unchanging and sovereign God, of course he does. His will cannot be thwarted, and there are those who are undeniably healed while on earth. But God heals according to his will and for his glory. Jesus lived with a "thy will be done" mentality throughout his life and ministry on earth. He even prayed those words as he prepared to suffer on the cross (Luke 22:42). Under the greatest weight a man has ever carried, and in preparation to take the sin of the world on his divine shoulders, God the Son submitted his will to the glorious plan and purpose of the Father's will. This is a model that should resonate with every believer today.

Can God heal? Yes. But sometimes he will glorify himself through your suffering, your sickness, and even your death. This counterintuitive way of thinking is foreign to this world. No wonder Peter called believers "foreigners" (1 Peter 2:11). We are a people called to an otherworldly perspective. We are different, even weird. Just think of how countercultural it is to believe that God will use your story for his glory no matter what the outcome may be. That is the greatest honor in this life. Greater even than physical healing in this life.

We're Just Getting Started

Earlier in the chapter, I told you that we'd discover truths about healing that would silence the lies you've been told. I hope you now see that you don't have to be lost and confused about Jesus and healing. More than that, you are not alone in your pain. Countless others are reading along with you—others who need the healing hand of Jesus to do what only he can do. And I am with you too as I write this for you. Certainly, Christyne and I cried out to God to heal our baby, Timothy, even while holding fast to the truths I have outlined in this chapter. We clung to

God's promises to be near the brokenhearted (Ps. 34:18) and to be our strength in times of weakness (2 Cor. 12:7–9). And we kept reminding ourselves to seek Jesus in all of this, to remember who he is and what he has already done for us.

What about you? What are you going through? Are you seeking to find Jesus and know him better, even in the midst of your trials? Do you know that Jesus is not only a healer? Of course you do. But isn't it so easy to forget? That's true for me. I can quickly get so caught up in what I want and my own suffering that I begin to neglect and even forget who Jesus is. So we're not done. Not even close! The best part of the book is the rest of it. Are you ready? Let's discover the rest of Jesus, the Jesus who is so much more than just a healer.

Questions for Reflection

1. Read John 9:1–34 and 1 Corinthians 11:27–30. Explain what these passages teach us about why some people are sick.
2. In what ways do you tend to love Jesus with a transactional love? Why doesn't transactional love build healthy relationships?
3. List some good things that you've seen come out of bad situations. How has God taken something dark and used it as a beacon of light? Pray for a renewed perspective on how God can work in the midst of pain. Meditate on Romans 8:28.
4. Why is it so important to pray "your will be done" kinds of prayers? How would you encourage someone who struggles to have this attitude of submission in prayer?

5. What is so dangerous about putting a price on healing? List several ways in which people can get hurt by this kind of teaching.

CHAPTER 2

HE IS PEACE

> *"Peace I leave with you; my peace I give you. I do not give to you as the world gives. Do not let your hearts be troubled and do not be afraid."*
>
> —JOHN 14:27

They say that money can't buy you happiness, but it can buy you peace of mind. If only that were true.

In the late 1800s, Horatio G. Spafford was known as one of Chicago's most successful lawyers and businessmen. Through the years his investments had paid off handsomely. In 1871 Mr. Spafford wrote to some of his friends that he felt he was "sitting on top of the world." He had a loving wife, four beautiful daughters, a profitable business empire, and a successful law practice.

But legend has it that one day a cow belonging to a woman

named Mrs. O'Leary kicked over a lantern in her barn. This ignited the Great Chicago Fire that killed many people, including some who attended the famous evangelist D. L. Moody's church service that same night. While the fire raged from Sunday, October 8, to Tuesday, October 10, 1871, Spafford's wealth was burned to ashes. He told his friends that all he had left of his business empire was his university diploma. Spafford's financial fall affected his wife hardest of all. Her doctor suggested that a vacation might help her. So Spafford arranged for a trip to Europe, but just prior to the departure, he received news about a pressing business matter in Chicago. He told his wife and daughters to go on ahead, and he planned to join them on a later ship.

Somehow, in the middle of the ocean, the ship carrying his wife and daughters collided with a British ship at full speed. In only twelve minutes, 226 people lost their lives. After the survivors reached Cardiff, Wales, Spafford received a two-word telegram from his wife that simply read, "Saved . . . alone."

Spafford booked the first ship bound for England. As he was sitting on the deck, the ship's captain informed him, "Mr. Spafford, we are approaching the spot where your daughters now rest." Instead of being grief-stricken as he had thought he would be, Spafford later recounted, a peace came over his mind as he remembered the words of his friend, D. L. Moody, who told him, "One of these days you are going to read that D. L. Moody of East Northfield is dead. Don't you believe a word of that; I'll be more alive than I am now."

As Spafford imagined his daughters more alive than they'd ever been, his heart exploded with words that replaced tears of sorrow with confident joy. Rushing to his cabin, Spafford wrote the words that had suddenly filled his heart.

> When peace, like a river, attendeth my way,
> When sorrows like sea-billows roll;
> Whatever my lot,
> Thou hast taught me to say,
> It is well, it is well with my soul.

In Spafford's greatest moment of pain, he found the greatest peace. As a result, he began to worship Jesus, and the rest of us were given one of history's greatest hymns. How is that possible? Because in a world full of uncertainty, doubt, fear, and loss, you find peace not by looking to yourself but by looking to Jesus.

The Gift That Money Can't Buy

I am convinced that nothing assaults our peace quite like sickness and the reality of death. No matter how much money we have, how successful we are, how well educated we've become, or how much we prepare, there are certain things we cannot protect ourselves from. In many ways, money is like the insulation in a house, and sickness or death is like a fire. Insulation can limit how warm we feel on a hot summer day or how cold we feel in the depths of winter, but if the house catches fire, insulation doesn't matter.

If you could package peace and turn it into a product, you'd quickly become the richest person on earth—probably even in all of history. People are constantly chasing down peace. I believe our quest for peace is linked to our survival instinct. We want to finally be at ease and know that our life is going to be comfortable. Like squirrels hoarding piles of nuts for winter, we believe that the more resources we have, the more likely we are to beat the elements, protect ourselves from peril, and survive. But is that how peace works? Gathering enough stuff until you feel peace? Can all the nuts in a forest protect a squirrel from a raging forest fire? No. Neither can all the money in the world save anyone from the brevity of life.

The Bible teaches that no one can truly have peace without the divine protection that Jesus provides. His protection is not for your stuff; it's for your soul. Best of all, it's free. It won't cost you any money. But there is one catch. It will cost you your loyalty to anything that you love more than Jesus. Jesus doesn't share. He wants your highest loyalty. The sad reality is, loyalty is where some people jump ship. To them, the peace that Jesus offers in exchange for their loyalty isn't worth it. We see this portrayed dramatically in the story of the rich young ruler.

I Won't Give *That* Up

Mark 10 tells the story about a rich young ruler who was likely experiencing earthly peace but perhaps was looking to add some eternal peace to his portfolio. The man inquired, "Good teacher, . . . what must I do to inherit eternal life?" (v. 17). Jesus responded, "Why do you call me good? . . . No one is good—except God alone" (v. 18). Jesus was letting this rich young ruler know that *good* should be used only to describe someone whose words were to be taken seriously. Was the rich young ruler using the term casually? Did he even understand what Jesus meant? We soon find out just how serious he is about listening to the good teacher.

Jesus said, "You know the commandments: 'You shall not murder, you shall not commit adultery, you shall not steal, you shall not give false testimony, you shall not defraud, honor your father and mother'" (v. 19). The rich ruler replied, "Teacher, . . . all these I have kept since I was a boy" (v. 20).

Simple enough, right? It sounds like the rich young ruler had everything going his way. Until Jesus went straight for his heart. Mark records this: "Jesus looked at him and loved him. 'One thing you lack,' he said. 'Go, sell everything you have and give to the poor, and you will have treasure in heaven. Then come, follow me.' At this the man's face fell. He went away sad, because he had great wealth" (vv. 21–22).

Whoa! Did Jesus just tell a man he could buy eternal life? It may seem like that's what happened, but we know that is completely outside of anything Jesus ever taught. On closer reflection, we see why Jesus made such an extreme statement. He was showing the man that even though he claimed to be keeping the law perfectly, he wasn't so perfect after all. The two greatest commandments are to love the Lord with all your heart and to love your neighbor as yourself (Matt. 22:37–40), but this man wasn't willing to do either. He wanted peace, but his hands were so full of his earthly desires that he couldn't receive the heavenly gift Jesus was offering. This rich man didn't love Jesus more than his money, even though Jesus looked upon him with such a deep and caring love, willing to offer him peace that would outlast anything his money could ever buy.

It's easy to scoff at the rich young ruler. What a blind fool! He couldn't get his eyes off his temporal desires for just one second to see the priceless treasure Jesus was offering. But what if we are just like that rich young ruler? What if we get so focused on our need for temporary peace that we forget that what we need most is eternal peace? And what if we think we're nailing it when it comes to religion, but we've relegated a relationship with Jesus to little more than a garnish on our main course? Is it possible that in our quest for peace, we are squarely focused on healing, financial success, a happy marriage, and a blossoming career, and treating Jesus as a throw-in?

If there is one thing that the story of the rich young ruler teaches us, it's this: to have the peace you need and the peace Jesus provides, you must love him more than anything else in this world. He is the anchor that can bring stability to your soul in the midst of the storm. He is the only one who can bring purpose out of your every pain, even if the breakthrough you've been praying for hasn't happened yet or doesn't happen at all.

God's Peace Is a Fact, Not a Feeling

To receive peace from God, you must first be at peace with God. People often make peace a subjective thing, saying, "I feel peace about this decision," or, "I don't want to do that because I don't feel peace about it." While there may be nothing wrong with wanting to feel peace, we need to make sure our feelings bow to our faith and to the facts in the Scriptures. The promises of God are not merely a feeling, they are a knowing!

One of my favorite preachers to listen to is Alistair Begg. He still possesses a brilliant Scottish accent even after pastoring a church in Cleveland for more than thirty years. Alistair tells a funny but helpful story about one Sunday when he visited a church in California. Looking forward to enjoying a Sunday off from the pulpit and to taking in the sights and sounds of another congregation, he eagerly waited for the service to begin. After an enthusiastic prelude, the worship leader burst forth with a question. "Hey! How do ya'll feel this morning?" Alistair's reaction? "What kind of question is that? If I told you how I feel, you'd question if I was even a Christian at all!"

Now, you may be a Sunday superstar, but for most of us, Alistair's response is the likeliest to resonate. Sunday can be a wild ride on the way to the pew. I can't help but surmise that how we feel is anything but excited as we run the gauntlet from our homes to church. Unruly kids, bathroom fights, spilled coffee, misplaced Sunday clothes, parking lot traffic, and putting on our best smile for the greetings . . . I think we all might echo what Alistair said next as he recalled the experience.

With Scottish gumption he roared, "Don't ask me that question. Ask me what I know! Don't ask me what I feel about myself. Ask me what I know about God. Ask me what I know about his Word. Ask me what I know to be a verity that can deal with my soul! That's what I need!"[4]

Those words ring true for every single one of us. We need the promises of God to fuel our hearts and minds, because our feelings so often fail us. We need to look to Jesus if we are to find peace in frantic times. We must be reminded that the Christian faith is not about feeling, it's about knowing. When it comes to peace, what Jesus offers is beyond anything this world could ever offer. His peace is beyond the comprehension of even the most brilliant minds.

When Jesus was preparing his disciples for the difficult times ahead, he said, "Peace I leave with you; my peace I give you. I do not give to you as the world gives. Do not let your hearts be troubled and do not be afraid" (John 14:27). Notice that Jesus said, "Do not let," pinpointing the core issue of how often we allow fear and anxiety to steal our peace. You may not *feel* like it, but you must *know* that Jesus has gifted you with the ability to stand firm against fear, worry, anxiety, and doubt so you can receive his perfect peace.

Why do you need to know and remember that Jesus is more than a healer? Because regardless of whether the healing comes, you're still going to need peace. And Jesus is the Prince of Peace (Isa. 9:6). Do you know peace? To really know it, you must know what God's Word promises about peace.

Jesus Is the Key to Peace for Your Soul

The Bible teaches a powerful truth regarding peace for the soul, in Romans 5:1–5. The apostle Paul writes, "Since we have been justified through faith, we have peace with God through our Lord Jesus Christ, through whom we have gained access by faith into this grace in which we now stand. And we boast in the hope of the glory of God. Not only so, but we also glory in our sufferings, because we know that suffering produces perseverance; perseverance, character; and character, hope. And hope does not put us to shame, because God's love has been poured out into our hearts through the Holy Spirit, who has been given to us."

This is peace in the midst of temporary pain. It's beyond human comprehension because it has divine origin. You can't get this peace by a feeling or by metaphysical strategies and positive thinking, as New Age gurus or prosperity gospel preachers will tell you. No amount of good thoughts will bring peace to your soul, unless those good thoughts are rooted in God saving your soul. If you have Jesus, when sickness, sorrow, or the armies of hell come to your very doorstep, nothing can steal away your peace. No pandemic, no peril, no persecution, no diagnosis can compare with what God is doing in you and through you when you stand on his promises for peace. The doctors may declare something is wrong with you, even terminally so, but if you have put your faith in Jesus Christ, then the Bible declares you are right with God.

Take courage; Jesus is your peace.

Jesus Is the Key to Peace in the Midst of Peril

Naturally, our response to the first promise the Bible makes about peace leads us to ask, "Okay! I've got eternal peace. But what about the peace I need right now when I feel so much anxiety about my situation?" Thankfully, the Bible speaks to that too.

Coaching a group of people who were challenged with tough times and suffering, the apostle Paul wrote, "Do not be anxious about anything, but in every situation, by prayer and petition, with thanksgiving, present your requests to God. And the peace of God, which transcends all understanding, will guard your hearts and your minds in Christ Jesus" (Phil. 4:6–7). When Christyne and I were battling the early onset of fear that accompanied Timothy's diagnosis, we found a new appreciation for Paul's words. Why would he tell Christians to not be anxious? Because it is quite normal to experience anxiety. We didn't have to feel guilt or shame for being anxious. We could openly confess it to the Lord. But we found it can also be quite normal to be liberated from anxiety and fear through the power of God's Word.

So we did the only thing we could think of to fulfill Paul's words in verse 8: "Finally, brothers and sisters, whatever is true, whatever is noble, whatever is right, whatever is pure, whatever is lovely, whatever is admirable—if anything is excellent or praiseworthy—think about such things." We put Scripture all over our house and used it to encourage each other in our conversations whenever anxiety and fear reared their ugly heads. We wrote up "Hinn Family Convictions" and had them printed and posted upstairs in our home. Christyne's friend Bre gave her a beautiful print of Psalm 61:2 that reads, "When my heart is faint, lead me to the rock that is higher than I." In Timothy's room, we hung a large, rustic wooden sign that a friend made for us which said, "And if not, He is still good" (based on Dan. 3:18). Like Shadrach, Meshach, and Abednego, we believed God could deliver us from the painful trial we faced, but we held fast to our conviction that Timothy's healing would not become an idol or a desire we demanded of God. I'll never forget coming home one day and walking up our stairwell and discovering a new sign Christyne had placed on the wall that faced the stairs so you couldn't miss it. Tears filled my eyes that day as I read the words of Job, who suffered far worse than we did: "He knows the way that I take; when he has tested me, I will come forth as gold" (Job 23:10). No matter the outcome, the Bible would be our backbone. Jesus would be our peace.

We didn't always do it perfectly, and some days we needed to read every sign in house just to get through. But before long the weight of fear and anxiety was lifting, and even more, it wouldn't linger very long whenever it came back. Why? Because God's Word is powerful. It is enough to renew your mind (Rom. 12:1–2).

When it comes to peace, it doesn't matter what you feel. It matters what you know. And what you know impacts how you live, how you pray, and how you stay grounded emotionally. Worry is ultimately a sin rooted in unbelief. When I am worried about outcomes, it's because I don't think God can handle my situation. What will I do? Who will help me? What will happen if there is conflict? How will I ever recover? The damage will be beyond repair! What about my future? What if I don't get healed right now? What about my money? What about my expectations? What about me, me, me and my worries!

Human comprehension strives for peace by thinking: I do. I control. I solve. But when we follow God's divine instructions for peace, it's guaranteed every time. The prophet Isaiah declares, "You will keep in perfect peace those whose minds are steadfast, because they trust in you. Trust in the LORD forever, for the LORD, the LORD himself, is the Rock eternal" (Isa. 26:3–4). That's a good word to remember whenever you're lacking peace.

Jesus Is the Key to Making Your Fears Flee

Hannah Hurnard, author of the devotional classic *Hinds' Feet on High Places*, was paralyzed by fear until she heard a sermon on scarecrows that challenged her to turn her fear into faith. In his sermon, the preacher said, "A wise bird knows that a scarecrow is simply an advertisement. It announces that some very juicy and delicious fruit is to be had for the picking. There are scarecrows in all the best gardens. . . . If I am wise, I too shall treat the scarecrow as though it were an invitation. Every giant in the way which makes me feel like a grasshopper is only a scarecrow beckoning me to God's richest blessings." He concluded, "Faith is a bird which loves to perch on scarecrows. All our fears are groundless."[5]

If you picture the "very juicy and delicious fruit" as the peace of God, and "God's richest blessings" as the hope of Christ through salvation, this is a perfect illustration for how often Satan tries to use fear to keep us from the greatest treasure we could ever have. He loves to try to guilt people into fear by lying about how hopeless they are in their sin and how they will never be good enough. He loves to try to get people to give up, by insisting that faith is useless for their impossible situation and that God would never love them enough to care. But he is dead wrong.

Whenever you begin to succumb to satanic lies, turn to Jesus in prayer. The power of prayer is the final key to peace. When Hannah was barren, she prayed (1 Sam. 1:9–26). When David ruined lives with his sin, he prayed (Psalm 51). When Esther risked death, she prayed (Est. 4:15–16). When Elijah needed a miracle, he prayed (1 Kings 18:36–37). When Jonah was swallowed by a fish, he prayed (Jonah 2:1–2). When Jesus was sweating blood, he prayed (Luke 22:42). When Paul had a "thorn in the flesh," he prayed (2 Cor. 12:7–10). Not all of those biblical characters were innocent in their circumstances, not all of them were at fault, and not all of them were rescued from their situation, but all received peace.

Try praying through the following four prayers and watch as fear flees and peace pours out over your heart and mind. Praying this way is kryptonite to the devil.

Prayer 1: Jesus, I Surrender Everything to You

James 4:7 gets straight to the point, telling us to "submit yourselves, then, to God. Resist the devil, and he will flee from you." I am convinced that we wallow in fear and lack peace because we don't put God's Word into practice. First Peter 5:6–7 instructs, "Humble yourselves, therefore, under God's mighty hand, that he may lift you up in due time. Cast all your anxiety on him because he cares for you." Notice that it doesn't say, "some anxieties." Or tell us to "slowly cast anxieties on God because he can't handle all of them at once." It says *all*. So why don't we? This is a great place for you and me to start, because it is the place of surrender. When we surrender ourselves to Jesus, we are saying, "My way doesn't work. I need you. Please help me. You are the solution. I give up." And why is that such a powerful way to unlock peace? Because God doesn't do pride, and pride can't live where surrender does. Just two verses before we're told to cast our anxieties on him, we're informed that God is not merely neutral toward prideful people but opposed to them (v. 5). Imagine having the God of the universe working against you. That equation will never equal peace. Pride says, "I can do this on my own." But faith says, "I can't do this without you, Jesus." And it is faith that pleases God (Heb. 11:6).

If you want the devil to flee, then put your faith in Jesus by surrendering your heart, mind, soul, will, and strength to Jesus. Admit you can't make it without him, then watch the incredible results unfold.

Prayer 2: Jesus, I Belong to You

The devil works overtime to make you doubt your salvation, because if you doubt your salvation, then you have no peace about eternity. It's not surprising that he attacks your eternal security, because for a Christian such assurance is paramount to eternal peace. If you've repented of sin, trusted Jesus in faith, and surrendered your life to him (prayer 1), then don't you dare give in to the lies of the enemy. Pray with confidence, and thank God for being your Father and Jesus for being your peace (Eph. 2:14).

You might be thinking, "But I just don't feel like I am perfect enough for Jesus yet." Well, join the club. Are any of us who we want to be? Absolutely not. But if we are genuine believers in

Jesus, then are we who we used to be? Not even close (2 Cor. 5:17). Begin to pray and thank God that you are saved, sealed, and set free from the bondage of sin, guilt, and death. Thank him for changing your mind, changing your heart, and changing your life. When you remember the truth about salvation and what it means to be a child of God, you (excuse the expression) "shut the devil up" because he has no more ammunition against you. Remember Romans 8:37–39? Well, so does he. Nothing "will be able to separate us from the love of God that is in Christ Jesus our Lord" (v. 39). With confidence you can recite Psalm 27:1, which declares, "The LORD is my light and my salvation—whom shall I fear? The LORD is the stronghold of my life—of whom shall I be afraid?"

My friend Dustin Benge tweeted it like this:

> Remember, when you think your faith will fail:
>
> 1. You are God's delight.
> 2. You are Christ's heir.
> 3. You are the Spirit's home.
> 4. You are Scripture's recipient.
> 5. You are heaven's citizen.[6]

What powerful reminders about the truth of who you belong to and the benefits of being a child of God. Praying this way unleashes the peace of God!

Prayer 3: Jesus, I Set My Mind on You

Did you know that spiritual warfare is a battle for your mind? People often imagine spiritual warfare as the devil showing up at the foot of your bed one night with a pitchfork, red horns, and a pointy tail, saying, "Here I am to get you!" But he's smarter than that. He knows that the way you think is linked to what you believe, and that what you believe will result in convictions that dictate how you live. So he goes for how we think. The Bible says that he tries to blind the minds of people to keep them from believing in Jesus. His goal is to rob us from having the greatest peace this world could ever know.

The solution to the devil's mind games is to have the "mind of Christ" (1 Cor. 2:16). Christians have the ability to think like Jesus. If we adopt his way of thinking, it will renew our minds and transform us so we stop dwelling on lies, negativity, gossip, fear, calamity, horror, and sin and start dwelling on what is true, honorable, right, pure, lovely, and good (Phil. 4:8–9). Jesus' way of thinking reflects the wisdom of God. That is why the Bible says to "let the word of Christ dwell in you richly" (Col. 3:16 ESV). When God's Word is flooding your mind, there is no room for the devil's lies.

But there is one problem: we don't think like Jesus perfectly. You and I give in to fear. We think the wrong things. Thankfully, just as confession to Jesus is the solution for the sins we hate doing but still do (Rom. 7:15; 1 John 1:9), there is a solution to the feeling that we're losing the battle for our minds. Read this powerful strategy from 2 Corinthians 10:4–5: "The weapons we fight with are not the weapons of the world. On the contrary, they have divine power to demolish strongholds. We demolish arguments and every pretension that sets itself up against the knowledge of God, and we take captive every thought to make it obedient to Christ."

Do you see the solution when you begin to falter in your

thinking? When thoughts enter your mind that are not in line with how Jesus would think, you don't need to shout at the devil or perform some mystical ritual. You simple pray, "Jesus, I am taking that thought captive right now and subjecting it to you. My sinful flesh thinks it knows best and thinks it can outsmart you, but I know who I belong to and the divine power that is in me to think like you do. I destroy that thought now and surrender my mind to you and your Word."

A Christian protects the mind, knowing it is the key to unfathomable peace.

Prayer 4: Jesus, I Rejoice with Thanksgiving No Matter What I Am Facing

This final prayer comes from a rejoicing heart that overflows with an attitude of gratitude. And yes, joy and thanksgiving may seem like the last two things on your mind when you're sinking in the sands of sickness and pain, but this approach is a key that unlocks perfect peace—even during imperfect circumstances.

In Philippians 4:4–7, we are told to rejoice, to have a kind spirit, to be anxious for nothing, and to pray about everything with thanksgiving. This results in peace that surpasses all comprehension and guards our hearts and minds in Christ Jesus. What a beautiful promise for a weary soul. When you rejoice in the Lord, have a Christ-centered perspective, and pray with an attitude of gratitude, the result is divine peace.

Thankful Christians are stable Christians because their joy isn't wrapped up in whether Jesus gives them what they want. For the believer, praying the right way about everything leads to peace about everything. You don't need pills to find peace, you need a prayer life. As you put these four prayers into practice, rest easy knowing that Jesus is near to you (Ps. 34:18) and is working even when you can't see immediate results.

God, Thank You for the Fleas

One of my favorite Christian heroes is a woman named Corrie ten Boom. She was a Dutch Christian who was the only member of her family to survive the concentration camps that Hitler and the Nazis set up to exterminate the Jews during World War II. Before her arrest, she and her family risked their lives to hide Jews from the Nazis. It wasn't long before she found herself in the most horrible place, alongside her sister Betsie.

Corrie's story is one of great heroism but also of earth-shattering sorrow. In her war-torn environment, we'd never think of finding an example of peace—let alone thanksgiving. Yet what Corrie learned in the midst of concentration camp horrors still proves to be a life raft of perspective for those who are drowning in pain. To learn from this heroine of history, we need to enter the Ravensbruck concentration camp and make our way to Barracks 28.

> Our noses told us, first, that the place was filthy. Somewhere plumbing had backed up, and the bedding was soiled and rancid. Then as our eyes adjusted to the gloom, we saw that there were no individual beds at all, but great square piers stacked three high, wedged side by side and end to end with an occasional narrow aisle slicing through.
>
> We followed our guide single file to the center of a large block. She pointed to the second tier. To reach it we had to stand on the bottom level, haul ourselves up, and then crawl

across three other straw-covered platforms to reach the one that we would share with—how many? The deck above us was too close to let us sit up. We lay back, struggling against the nausea that swept over us from the reeking straw. We could hear other women finding their places.

Suddenly I sat up, striking my head on the cross-slats above. Something had pinched my leg.

"Fleas!" I cried. "The place is swarming with them!"

We scrambled across the platforms, heads low to avoid another bump, dropped down to the aisle, and edged our way to the patch of light.

"Betsie, how can we live in such a place?" I wailed.

"Show us how." It was said so matter of factly it took me a second to realize she was praying. The distinction between prayer and the rest of life seemed to be vanishing for Betsie.

"Corrie!" she said excitedly. "In the Bible this morning. Where was it? Read that part again!"

I glanced down the long dim aisle to make sure no guard was in sight, then drew the Bible from its pouch. "It was in First Thessalonians," I said. "Here it is: 'Comfort the frightened, help the weak, be patient with everyone. See that none of you repays evil for evil, but always seek to do good to one another and to all.'"

"Go on," said Betsie.

"Oh, yes. 'To one another and to all. Rejoice always, pray constantly, give thanks in all circumstances—'"

"That's it, Corrie! That's His answer, 'Give thanks in all circumstances!' That's what we can do. We can thank God for everything about this new barracks!"

I stared at her, then around at the foul-aired room.

"Such as?" I said.

"Such as being assigned here together."

I bit my lip. "Oh, yes, Lord Jesus!"

"Such as what you're holding in your hands."

I looked down at the Bible. "Thank You, dear Lord, that there was no inspection when we entered here! Thank You for all the women, here in this room, who will meet You in these pages."

"Yes," said Betsie. "Thank You for the very crowding here. Since we're packed so close, that many more will hear!" She looked at me expectantly.

"Oh, all right," I said. "Thank You for the jammed, crammed, packed, suffocating crowds."

"Thank You," Betsie went on, "for the fleas and for—"

This was too much. "Betsie, there's no way even God can make me grateful for a flea."

"'Give thanks in all circumstances,'" she quoted. "Fleas are part of this place where God has put us."

So we gave thanks for the fleas.[7]

Betsie and Corrie soon discovered that the fleas were the reason why no soldier and not even a supervisor would deign to enter Barracks 28. Because of the infestation of one of God's smallest creatures, Bible studies, worship, fellowship, and prayer could go on unhindered.

In the midst of your sickness, pain, and uncertainty, perhaps there are fleas in your life that you can thank God for. Maybe your situation has opened doors to share the gospel. Or maybe you've prayed more than ever before because of your brokenness. Never forget, your knees are the safest place to be in your darkest hour. Could it be that peace is just a prayer away? Jesus is ready to provide it. Ask and you will receive it.

Questions for Reflection

1. List a few truths from this chapter that encouraged and/or challenged you.
2. Keeping you from prayer is one of the key ways that the devil tries to steal your peace. What are some barriers to your prayer life that keep you from setting aside time to spend with the Lord? How will you overcome those?
3. Some people turn to their net worth, shopping ("retail therapy"), physical fitness, or a successful career to obtain peace. How would you encourage someone who is thriving to still look to Jesus as the ultimate peace?
4. Why is using alcohol or drugs to numb our pain a poor substitute for looking to Jesus?
5. The problem with the rich young ruler (Mark 10:17–22) was not that he was rich but that he loved his riches more than he loved Jesus. List some competing loves that you're determined to keep second to Jesus. These could even be good things like kids, a thriving career, or affirmation from others. Pray over these with a spouse, friend, or small group and seek accountability concerning them.

CHAPTER 3

HE IS SAVIOR

> *"As a shepherd looks after his scattered flock when he is with them, so will I look after my sheep. I will rescue them from all the places where they were scattered on a day of clouds and darkness."*
>
> —EZEKIEL 34:12

Now that we've had two chapters to give us a foundational perspective, it's time for a comforting yet challenging step deeper into the truth about Jesus. If you and I are going to grow closer to the Jesus we truly need, we must not merely accept this next truth on a surface level but also embrace it in the depths of our soul. Here it is: healing for your body is not as important as healing for your soul.

At first glance this statement can sting because it seems to overlook our most pressing and human need, especially if we're sick or praying for someone who is. But as we walk through this chapter, you will find that it is one of the most comforting realities you and I could ever embrace.

Jesus Said What?

Sadly, in many churches today people are consistently sold the lie that Jesus' main goal is your perfect health, wealth, and happiness. It's not that those things are bad things, but they are not the main thing.

In the first chapter of the gospel of Mark, the author wastes no time plunging readers right into Jesus' powerful healing ministry. By the time we reach verse 29, Jesus has been baptized by John the Baptist and a voice from heaven has called him a "beloved Son" (vv. 9–11 ESV), he has called people to follow him and become his disciples (vv. 16–20), he has taught with unprecedented authority (vv. 21–22), and he has commanded an evil spirit to obey him (vv. 23–28). Jesus is a big deal, and for good reason. It isn't long before he is healing people left and right, and the crowds line up with their sick and demon-possessed loved ones, looking for the Healer to give them what they want most (vv. 29–34). Being the compassionate and divine Son of God, Jesus heals them and sets them free with such undeniable results that even his enemies can see that he has real power. Yet the next day Jesus makes a remarkable statement to his disciples. "Very early in the morning, while it was still dark, Jesus got up, left the house and went off to a solitary place, where he prayed. Simon and his companions went to look for him, and when they found him, they exclaimed: 'Everyone is looking for you!' Jesus replied,

'Let us go somewhere else—to the nearby villages—so I can preach there also. That is why I have come'" (vv. 35–38).

In Luke's parallel passage, Jesus says, "I must proclaim the good news of the kingdom of God to the other towns also, because that is why I was sent" (Luke 4:43). What does Jesus mean? Does he not care about the sick any longer? Is he tired of meeting the physical needs of the hurting? Not at all. From the evidence of his entire ministry and the underlying purpose of every parable, every miracle, and his sacrifice on the cross, Jesus most certainly healed throughout his ministry and still does today, but he still was focused on one thing above everything else. His purpose wasn't merely healing people from sickness or setting them free from demons. It was saving them from sin and eternal death and separation from God.

While nowhere in any of the gospels or the rest of the New Testament does Jesus or the apostles negate miracles or denigrate healing, all through the gospels and the New Testament we see the saving power of Jesus Christ held up as the primary focus (or the true why) behind his coming to earth. Jesus said, "The Son of Man came to seek and to save the lost" (Luke 19:10). Paul said, "I resolved to know nothing while I was with you except Jesus Christ and him crucified" (1 Cor. 2:2). John said, "I write these things to you who believe in the name of the Son of God so that you may know that you have eternal life" (1 John 5:13). Again, none of this diminishes God's love or power to heal you on earth. Rather it should elevate your view of his love and power because it showcases his desire to be with you in heaven.

God can heal from anywhere. He can heal at any time. But theologically speaking, in order to reconcile sinners to himself, he had to send his Son to earth to be a perfect and blameless blood sacrifice that would satisfy God's holy wrath toward sin and save the sinner. Jesus was that perfect and blameless blood sacrifice. He came down so we could go up. He was humbled so we could be exalted. He gave his life so we could live forever.

You can have all the miracles your heart desires, but without Jesus saving your soul, you will miss out on the greatest miracle of all. You can be healed of every disease, but like every single human being to ever live, you will eventually die (Heb. 9:27). The plain fact is that you need healing for the sickness of sin more than anything. For what does it profit anyone if they gain the world yet lose their soul, or what does it profit anyone to be healed of disease, experience relational breakthroughs, and achieve professional success if they lose their soul (Mark 8:36)? The glory of heaven awaits those who put their faith in Jesus Christ alone. Your life on earth is but a grain of sand when compared with the endless shores of eternity. It's okay to want relief from whatever you're going through, but most important is where you're going to.

When enduring any type of trial in life, remember why the Savior came. Is he yours?

The Danger of Eye-Rolling the Savior

If you're normal, or just human, you may be struggling with this thought: "Thanks for the pleasantries and platitudes about salvation and Jesus. I agree, but I want my healing now. I want my best life now. Give me the solution for that."

Perhaps that thought is a caricature or exaggerated, but some form of it takes shape in all our minds from time to time. We may want eternity in heaven, but we want all of the benefits now.

Without our temporary relief, we grow discontented. So much so that we may even be tempted to dump Christianity altogether if it doesn't deliver the results we're seeking.

This is precisely what the devil wants you to do. He cheers when you eye-roll messages about heaven. He longs for you to dismiss biblical truths that challenge your temporary perspective and to focus only on seeking out quick fixes and shallow pursuits. If he has his way, you'll go straight for quick-fix drugs, like the prosperity gospel, in your search for instant gratification—even if they don't deliver the long-term goods. As so many physical drugs are designed to do, this spiritual drug will fill you up for a moment with relief or euphoria, then send you crashing into despair, needing another hit.

That may sound harsh, but hear me out. It doesn't matter where you're reading this or who you are, love for souls transcends distance, and God is no respecter of persons (Acts 10:34). He doesn't want any of us to hold back truth from one another, especially truth that helps us grow closer to him. If you are a human being, you are made in the image of God, and I care too much about you to hold back in this section. Love compels me to tell you the sobering truth. I refuse to let you go through this book, or this life, without hearing this: if Jesus' being your Savior isn't enough for you, you are in serious, spiritual danger.

Think for a moment about the Pharisees. How often do we pick on them for their super spiritual religiosity and rule making and because they were the ultimate hypocrites? Admittedly, they are an easy target because of how rude they were to Jesus and how hard they were on people. Surely we have nothing in common with them. Or do we?

Seeking Signs instead of the Savior

In another confrontation with the religious leaders of his day, Jesus made a serious accusation. He told them they were missing the most important fact—that he was the Savior—and instead were seeking signs and wonders. The religious leaders demanded a sign from Jesus. But Jesus answered, "A wicked and adulterous generation asks for a sign! But none will be given it except the sign of the prophet Jonah" (Matt. 12:39). These people kept chasing down Jesus and insisting he perform signs and do their bidding, yet they didn't even believe that he was the Savior! In response Jesus declared they'd be given the "sign of Jonah," which was a reference to Jonah being in the belly of a fish for three days and coming out—just as Jesus would be in the grave for three days and then come out. The religious leaders got Jesus crucified, only to beget the greatest miracle in the history of the universe, when Jesus rose from the dead. In contrast to the people of Nineveh, who repented when Jonah told them God's message, most of the sign-seeking religious leaders continued in their superficial spirituality. They saw miracles, they witnessed healings, but instead of believing in the Savior, they crucified him.

Their blindness is a lesson to us to never let the signs and wonders we want get in the way of our seeking the Savior we need.

Throughout history there are many lessons to be learned from people who vigorously sought something that eluded them in the end because that thing they were seeking could not satisfy the deeper longing in their soul. Look at this list compiled by Donald McCullough in his article "The Pitfalls of Positive Thinking."

- Alexander the Great conquered Persia but broke down and wept because his troops were too exhausted to push on to India.
- Hugo Grotius, the father of modern international law, said at the last, "I have accomplished nothing worthwhile in my life."
- John Quincy Adams, sixth president of the US—not a Lincoln, perhaps, but a decent leader—wrote in his diary, "My life has been spent in vain and idle aspirations, and in ceaseless rejected prayers that something would be the result of my existence beneficial to my species."
- Robert Louis Stevenson wrote words that continue to delight and enrich our lives, yet what did he write for his epitaph? "Here lies one who meant well, who tried a little, and failed much."
- Cecil Rhodes opened up Africa and established an empire, but what were his dying words? "So little done, so much to do."[8]

How could leaders who managed to etch their names in history and who seemed to accomplish so much throughout their lives be so empty in the end? It's impossible to know everything they were thinking, but I believe it is because they came to realize that death is the great equalizer. No matter what they were seeking, no matter what they accomplished, no matter who they became, they too had an expiration date that could not be altered. They came to grips with their finite insignificance. All human beings who have lived, who are living, and who will live are going to breathe their last one day. The only solution to feelings of despair is to find rest in the firm grip of the Savior. This life is but a vapor. Eternity is forever. Do you have hold of the Savior? Better yet, does the Savior have hold of you?

So what now?

Realize What Matters Most Is Your Salvation

When the apostle Peter was encouraging the early church in the midst of extreme difficulties, he commended them for the way they were looking to Jesus, loving him and believing in him even though they had never seen him. He explained to them that because they were seeking him, their ultimate reward would be obtaining the outcome of their faith, which was the salvation of their souls (1 Peter 1:8–9). I find encouragement like this fascinating because it is so counterintuitive to the way we think today. Was Peter promising the church an easy escape from their pain? Was he guaranteeing them double for their trouble? No. His encouragement was not of this world. Rather it involved their total assurance of the glory of heaven and the realization of all that they believed. Peter, the apostle who could heal, who could deliver, who could cast out demons, and who had physically been with Jesus wasn't promising his readers exemption from physical suffering and death. He was reminding them that by having faith in the Savior, they were living the "now but not yet." It was a done deal. They could count on it. Instead of empty regrets in death, they could have joy knowing that they were going to meet their Savior. I want you to have such assurance. Like Peter's readers, you may not have what you want, but if you have Jesus as your Savior, you have everything you need.

How to Know the Savior

I've told you that Jesus is the Savior, I've shown you Scripture passages that tell you he is the Savior, but how does he *become* your Savior?

The Bible teaches first that God initiates the process of Jesus becoming your Savior. Jesus said in John 6:44, "No one can come to me unless the Father who sent me draws them." In plain terms, Jesus was explaining that the first step in salvation is that God begins to stir a desire in your heart for him.

Perhaps you remember when this happened in your life, or perhaps it even started to happen as you read this book looking for answers and hope. Whatever the case, the Bible clearly teaches that God begins to draw you from the inside, and then from the outside you hear (or read) what it means to have faith in Jesus. Romans 10:17 says, "Faith comes from hearing the message, and the message is heard through the word about Christ." Again, the Bible makes it easy to understand. You come to believe in Jesus by something powerful happening inside you when the powerful message of "Jesus as Savior" comes to you from the outside.

Within that message, some key truths must be conveyed and believed. You might say that the following truths answer the question, what in the world am I saved from? Or, why in the world do I need a Savior?

1. You are a sinner and have fallen short of God's perfect standard. You are not perfect and never will be (Rom. 3:23).
2. The penalty for any and all sin is death. This is because God has determined it to be so. His standard for

relationship must be perfection, because he is perfect. Because of our sin, we deserve to be punished with eternal separation from God (Rom. 6:23).

3. In his kindness, mercy, and love, God sent his Son, Jesus, to die in our place as a perfect sacrifice which would satisfy the wrath of God and pay the penalty for sin (Rom. 5:8; 2 Cor. 5:17–21). When Jesus was raised from the dead after three days in the grave, he proved that he was God and able to atone for our sins.
4. All those who place their faith in Jesus Christ are forgiven and covered by his blood. When you confess that you are a great sinner and that Jesus is a great Savior, and you believe that he was and is the Son of God, you will be saved and can never be condemned for your sin and separated from God (John 3:16; Rom. 5:1; 8:1). Those who are in Christ are protected by his sacrifice (2 Cor. 5:17) and live a new life dedicated to following him. Literally nothing can separate you from God's love if you believe in Jesus Christ (Rom. 8:38–39).

This is the treasure of salvation: assurance that Jesus has you and you have him. In the letter of Philippians, the apostle Paul writes about the great value in knowing Christ, saying, "Whatever gain I had, I counted as loss for the sake of Christ. Indeed, I count everything as loss because of the surpassing worth of knowing Christ Jesus my Lord" (Phil. 3:7–8 ESV). In Romans 8:18, he exclaims, "I consider that our present sufferings are not worth comparing with the glory that will be revealed in us." Both of these passages are further evidence that the God of the Bible has more for you on the other side of this life than you could ever imagine. Being saved is more important than being healed. Having Jesus is more important than having anything money could buy. Deliverance from your sin is more important than deliverance from suffering.

Maybe you're reading this and thinking, "I'm not sick or suffering right now, so how might any of this apply to me?" To you, the same truths apply. Are there things that are more important to you than your salvation? It could be:

- a happy marriage
- a high-paying job
- obedient kids
- the perfect neighborhood
- a stylish home
- your social status
- being liked by others

Is it possible that some of these good things in life are what you are truly seeking, and Jesus is more of a cherry on top than anything else? If you didn't have Jesus but you had everything on that list, would you be fine?

No matter your station in life, I encourage you to reexamine the affections of your heart and commit to believing that even if everything was going wrong in your life but you had Jesus, then the most important thing would still be going right.

Steal Away to Jesus

Thomas Lewis Johnson was a brave and heroic preacher who achieved his dream of preaching the gospel in Africa. He was a man with God-given boldness, humility, and incredible perseverance. Life was no easy road for Thomas. Before he became a preacher, he was born into slavery and lived as a slave for twenty-eight years. At just three years old, he was cruelly taken from his mother, who was also a slave, and he wouldn't see her again until the age of nine. His masters were terribly hard on their slaves. Deep down their brutality was rooted in cowardice; they feared that their slaves would someday adopt a mind of their own and realize how strong they were. In an effort to suppress any thoughts of freedom or strength, they beat their slaves, including Thomas. He longed for freedom. He thought about it day and night for more than two decades. The pain he endured is something few could imagine today. Yet there amid the horrors of slavery, God used another slave, named Ezekiel, to reveal to Thomas a freedom that no man could suppress. Thomas found that no matter how hard they tried to crush his body, no slave owner could crush the soul.

One night as he was lying in bed and lost in hopeless despair, Thomas recalled the words that Ezekiel once spoke to him: "I'm telling you, boy, you're looking for freedom in all the wrong places." He wondered if those words were true. If so, how? Thomas could bear his despair no longer. He got out of bed, risking a beating (or worse) from the plantation foreman, and went to find Ezekiel in his sleeping quarters. Upon his arrival, Thomas found Ezekiel huddled in a circle with several others, singing these words:

> Steal away, Steal away.
> Steal away to Jesus;
> Steal away, Steal away home;

> I ain't got long to stay here.
>
> So steal away, Steal away to Jesus.

Authors Matt Carter and Aaron Ivey beautifully describe what happened next as the group of slaves, led by Ezekiel, moved from singing to talking about Jesus. But not before Ezekiel caught Thomas peering through the window and motioned for him to come inside and join them. He did.

> "I got one question for each of you tonight," whispered Ezekiel as he looked directly at Thomas. Even in the darkness of the room, Thomas could see his friend's eyes—bright and piercing—speaking to everyone, but looking only at him.
>
> "Have you stolen away to Jesus?" Ezekiel paused, letting the question soak in.
>
> "Have you stolen away from this place—your work, your troubles—have you gotten alone with the Lord? 'Cause that might be the most important question you answer all day long. 'Cause you see, the master . . . he owns our body. The master, he owns our time. The master, he owns everything about us," Ezekiel continued to whisper, looking only to Thomas.
>
> "But. There is something you can't ever forget. There is one thing that man don't own. There is one thing that man can't ever own.
>
> "He don't own the soul."
>
> Several of the slaves moaned quietly in agreement, gently rocking back and forth to the slow, rhythmic cadence of the whispering preacher. "There is another Master. And this Master—He is the real Master of this whole world. He's the One that your soul *really* belongs to. His name is Jesus. . . .

> "But here's the Good News—you can be free. Really free. Right here. Right now. No matter where you are. No matter what you do. No matter what kinda chains you carryin' with you."[9]

That very night, on a Virginia plantation, Thomas Johnson sat drinking in every single word that Ezekiel preached and came to realize that if no one ever removed his physical chains, Jesus would shatter his spiritual ones. Every injustice that could steal his human right to freedom could never stop his right to freedom as a child of God. Every bondage on earth could do nothing to stop the blessing of heaven. Every limit to his earthly inheritance could not stop the eternal riches that were his through Jesus Christ. There in a huddle of slaves, the explosive power of God transcended the malicious power of their master. Thomas put his faith in Jesus Christ.

Almost ten years after that night, he saw the Lord set him free from the chains of slavery. Even more, he was invited by Charles Spurgeon to complete his education at the Pastor's College in London. This served as a catalyst to his achieving his dream of preaching in Africa. Thomas Johnson's freedom from slavery, and his opportunities to live the remainder of his life on earth with glorious purpose, was a great treasure to him. But even until his dying breath, he considered his freedom from sin at the hands of the Savior to be the greatest treasure of all.[10]

How Do I Know If I Am Saved?

As we close out this chapter, I want you to have complete confidence in your salvation. Every child of God deserves to have assurance of eternal joy, even if they're enduring temporal pain.

One of my favorite passages is Romans 1:16, which says, "I am not ashamed of the gospel, because it is the power of God that brings salvation to everyone who believes." That word *believes,* in the way that the apostle Paul uses it, indicates a continuous action. The power of the gospel will transform people's lives, and they will keep on believing and living for Jesus. What a relief that the power to stay saved isn't in our hands, it's in God's.

If you genuinely believe something, you won't just say you believe it. Your actions will back up your words. The Bible is clear that you are not saved by good works, but you are saved *for* good works (Eph. 2:8–10). Jesus told his disciples, "If you love me, keep my commands" (John 14:15). James tells us that faith without works is dead (James 2:17) and that even the demons believe in God (v. 19). If you're really saved, your life is going to start to look different and bear the evidence of a transformed heart and mind. To help you feel confident about your faith, here are ten things that will start to become evident in the life of a person who has Jesus as their Savior. If you don't see these as much as you'd like in your life, this closing section of the chapter is the perfect opportunity to cry out to Jesus and ask him to be your Savior.

1. *You confess Jesus Christ as your Lord and Savior and trust in him by faith (Rom. 10:9).* Every true believer must come to Christ declaring, "You are God! Your way is better. My way doesn't work. I need you. I believe in you. I trust in you by faith for my salvation. I will follow you for the rest of my life." Have you believed in your heart and confessed with your mouth that Jesus Christ is Lord?
2. *You confess sin; you are no longer indifferent toward it*

(*1 John 1:9*). True believers care about sin, not because they like committing it but because they want to deal with it. Confession of sin is evidence of genuine faith. Those who are following Jesus bring their sin and shame to his feet, claiming, "I repent! I hate this sin that keeps waging war against my soul. Please forgive me. Help me escape it."

3. *Habitual patterns of sin are decreasing and fading (1 Cor. 6:11; 2 Cor. 5:17).* If you're a new creation, you're not going to look old for long. Genuine faith transforms us. When the Bible lists horrible sins and says things like, "Such were some of you" (1 Cor. 6:11 ESV), the genuine believer can joyously say, "Yes, that *was* me!" I like to say it like this: "I'm still not who I'm going to be, but I am definitely not who I used to be."
4. *You desire to be obedient to Christ (James 1:22).* If you truly desire to follow Jesus and he has won victory in your heart, you're not just going to want to hear the Word of God, you're going to want to do it.
5. *Your love for others is increasing (1 John 3:14).* "Hateful Christian" is an oxymoron. Yes, being a follower of Jesus means speaking truth no matter the cost, but that is always to be done in love (Eph. 4:15). More than that, true believers are marked by a love for others that goes way beyond what they say, it's about what they do.
6. *You hunger for God's Word (1 Peter 2:2).* A genuine love for Jesus and a true conversion of your soul is going to result in a passionate hunger to know what he has said and what he has called you to do. True Christians are not indifferent to God's Word.

7. *You are filled with a desire to see others saved (2 Cor. 5:18–20).* People who have been reconciled to God want to see others reconciled to him as well. It's that simple. Do you have a deep desire to be an ambassador for Christ? That is evidence of his work in your heart.
8. *You love to serve the body of Christ with good works (Eph. 2:10; 1 Peter 4:7–11).* There is no such thing as lone ranger Christianity or a genuine belief that does not want to genuinely serve. Good works are not *required* for salvation, they are the *result* of salvation. Christians are given spiritual gifts to build up the body of Christ. When we desire to use our gifts to serve others, we are living out real faith.
9. *You experience the discipline of God (Heb. 12:6–8; Ps. 11:5).* This may seem crazy, but when God disciplines you, it means that he loves you. Only a cruel parent lets their child run into harm's way. God's correction is done with love. Like a gracious Father, he is not content to let his children continue in sin that harms them. He guides the truly saved as a faithful shepherd guides his sheep, even if that means using the staff sometimes to correct their crooked path.
10. *You are bearing the fruit of the Spirit (Luke 6:43; Gal. 5:22–23).* Bad trees don't produce good fruit. Good trees don't produce bad fruit. So it is for people as well. A fake Christian will be known by false fruit or no fruit at all. A genuine believer will look at the list in Galatians 5:22–23 and by God's grace rejoice, saying, "My life looks like that more than it used to!" One day, they will see God finish the work he began in them, when their earthly life ends and they meet Christ face-to-face (Phil. 1:6).

It may be hard to face certain realities in your life, but the wise and prudent Christian finds comfort in Paul's words: "Examine yourselves to see whether you are in the faith; test yourselves. Do you not realize that Christ Jesus is in you—unless, of course, you fail the test?" (2 Cor. 13:5).

No matter what burdens you are carrying, I want you to unload the heavy burden of doubt when it comes to your salvation. If you trust Jesus as your Savior, nothing—not cancer, bankruptcy, abuse, persecution, pain, or any other calamity—can stop the bounty that awaits you in heaven. He *is* Savior. Is he yours?

Questions for Reflection

1. List a few truths from this chapter that encouraged and/or challenged you.
2. In your own words, explain why healing for the soul is more important than healing for the body.
3. When we are experiencing pain or trials in life, it can be a challenge to see something like salvation as more important than relief of our suffering. What passages from Scripture can encourage us to develop an eternal perspective?
4. Read the following passages and write down what each one says about how a person may come to faith in the Savior.
   a. Matthew 4:17
   b. Romans 10:9
   c. Romans 10:17
   d. Ephesians 2:8–10
   e. Revelation 3:20

5. Do you see the evidences of God's powerful work in your life? Which ones from the list at the end of the chapter are most obvious? What ones are you trusting the Lord to keep growing in you?

CHAPTER 4

HE IS HOPE

> *We have this hope as an anchor for the soul, firm and secure.*
>
> —HEBREWS 6:19

In 1927, just off the shore of Massachusetts, a US submarine was accidentally rammed by a US Coast Guard ship, causing it to sink with the entire crew of forty men trapped inside. Every effort was made to rescue the crew, but rescuers struggled to find a way into the submarine without drowning everyone inside. Nearing the end of the ordeal, with oxygen running low, a deep-sea diver was circling the sub and heard a tapping sound. He placed his head against the sub and began making sense of the Morse code being tapped on the walls of the sub from the inside. He translated it in his mind and the message was, "Is . . . there . . . any . . . hope?" The message came from one of six remaining crew members still alive, but barely. The rescuers responded, "There is hope. Everything possible is being done." Sadly, however, their best efforts were stymied by the weather, and the last six crew members also perished.

Have you ever felt that way in life? Trapped? Holding on by a thread? Suffocating in a sea of burdens? If you're reading this book, either you or people you know feel that way right now.

When we look at the news cycle, it seems like all we see is hopelessness. Like a burgeoning stock market, certain things are up, but they aren't the things that give us hope. Domestic abuse is up. Child abuse is up. Pornography and sex trafficking are up. Political division is up. Suicide rates are up. Fear is up.

The concept of death and feelings of despair can be crippling to our hope. People don't want to talk about death, let alone contemplate it. Sickness is something we greatly fear not only because of the pain and discomfort it brings but also because of the terminal results it can cause. Have you ever walked the cancer ward in a hospital? Have you ever sat with a family as the doctors explain there is nothing more they can do? If you have, you've seen the crushing weight of hopelessness. Yet Jesus can take crushing weight and turn it into a catalyst for hope. Whether you struggle with depression, thoughts of suicide, or terminal illness—or know someone who does—this chapter is the anthem of hope that roars, "You are not alone!" For the Christian, hope is not a distant dream, it can be a daily reality. Hope is not blind optimism. Hope is a realist. Hope knows that things may be hard, outcomes may be horrid, and relief may be out of reach, but hope knows something else too.

When the question comes, "Is there any hope?" the answer that you must come to know and proclaim to others is a resounding, "Yes!" There is hope. No matter what hell you're enduring, Jesus is hope. No matter what hurts need healing, Jesus is hope. No matter what hindrance you're facing, Jesus is hope. He is the one who has overcome every trouble in this world and can guarantee you hope in the midst of hopelessness.

A Lesson from Early Christians

As we unpack life-changing truths together in this chapter, I need you to put on your Bible nerd hat for a few hundred words. I promise this is going to make sense. Stick with me here.

In the New Testament letter of 1 Peter, we find truths written to a scattered group of believers in what is now Turkey who were suffering and in desperate need of hope. When Peter wrote to these Christians, he was likely in Rome and the church was about to experience the persecutions that made him a martyr in AD 64. The emperor of Rome at the time was Nero. Evidence suggests that he was behind the fire that destroyed Rome, but he needed to lay the blame somewhere in order to keep the focus off him. Christians were the perfect scapegoat because their religious zeal annoyed both Jews and Romans, so he blamed them. Soon hatred for Christians increased and immense suffering and senseless killing began. Some Christians were torn apart by dogs, while others were burned like torches, and still others—including Peter—were crucified. Such crimes against humanity can barely be imagined, let alone fathomed. Why do I bring that up? Because amid this increasing persecution of believers, Peter presented one of the most jaw-dropping and challenging calls for hope ever.

The apostle Peter, the same one who would be crucified by

Nero, commanded Christians facing trials and persecution to set their hope fully on the grace that would be brought to them when Jesus returned (1 Peter 1:13).

This was a command to hope in what is ahead and to lay aside every other hope. If your hope is going to thrive, you must tie your emotions and your soul to the anchor of Christ. Set your course by his commands. Set your hope completely on the day you will meet him face-to-face, and stay focused on why you're here on earth. This world is not your home. You're just passing through. Your outlook determines your outcome. What you live for, you will live out. And your outlook and what you're living for must be all wrapped up in Jesus if you're going to have hope that outlasts the challenges this life throws your way.

Be like the man who was losing his memory and went to his doctor for advice. He received this diagnosis from the doctor: "We cannot help your memory without impairing your eyesight. Now the choice is yours. Would you rather be able to see or to remember?" The man thoughtfully replied, "Frankly, I'd rather have my eyesight than my memory, because I'd rather see where I'm going than remember where I've been."

Are you looking to Jesus? Anticipating his return? Seeking his glory? Now apply that to your weary soul and heavy mind. Maybe you have cancer, maybe you are going through a painful divorce or financial crisis, maybe you're watching your child fight for his or her life, or maybe you're wrestling with unanswered questions about the future, like we are when it comes to our son, Timothy. Friends, let's lift up our eyes! Where does our help come from? Our help comes from the Lord, who made heaven and earth (Ps. 121:1–2). In the same way that Peter encouraged the early church, I want to encourage you—even challenge you—to set your hope fully on what God has in store for you. Let that word *fully* be the standard for your hope. Because of the gospel, commit to looking forward to Jesus coming back, commit to believing that he can take your pain and turn it into purpose, and commit to trusting that he will have the final say in your situation, even if that is in heaven.

Five Hope Breakers

As a pastor, I engage with thousands of people every year in both formal and informal settings. From church members and local government leaders to parachurch workers and new believers, many people generously share their wisdom and experiences, and I glean a great deal from those conversations. As much as it is a privilege to interact with so many people and learn from their stories, it can be equally as heartbreaking. It seems that no matter where I go or who I am talking to, I meet countless people (whether they are newer or older Christians) who struggle with hopelessness.

None of us are immune to challenges that try to steal our hope. I call these challenges hope breakers because they tend to break down our hope. Before we know it, we find it hard to find joy, peace, and of course hope. And when we can't find hope, it's even harder to love. Many of the angriest people you'll ever meet are expressing an emotion rooted in hopelessness. They don't see the light at the end of the tunnel, and in some way, shape, or form they snap. Some don't see even a glimpse of hope in their life, while others have hope for eternity but wrestle with having hope for their marriage, job, or ministry. Whatever the case, we do well to enumerate these hope breakers so we can better understand and appreciate the hope builders that God provides for us.

I'm sure you could add more, but these five hope breakers are categorized according to what I most frequently encounter.

Hope Breaker 1: When We Don't Know God

I believe that deep down in the soul of every person who does not know God is an insecurity that only God can solve. Some years ago a newly married couple contacted our church for pastoral counseling for their marriage. Within a few days the couple was in my office, and the wife was hysterical. She had one idea about marriage; the husband had an entirely different idea. She thought something was terribly wrong. He thought nothing was wrong at all. They began to shout at each other, and eventually they turned on me. She was leaning over my desk, screaming, "You better fix this or it's hopeless!" After a few choice expletives were directed at me and then at her husband, I asked her to calm down and followed up with two simple questions.

"Do you two even attend our church?"

They replied, "No."

"Are you two even Christians?"

They both shook their heads.

I began to explain that I could offer some general counsel but that the situation was going to be hopeless unless they knew God and put their faith in Jesus Christ. After I spent several minutes trying to share the gospel with them, they wanted nothing more than to avoid the Bible and any talk about Jesus. She stormed out. The young man shrugged his shoulders and followed her.

This story is a simple illustration of how hopeless we truly are unless we know God. They wanted solutions without a Savior. It's impossible to have true and lasting hope when you don't have a higher power in your corner. What a hope breaker! Imagine having to walk around every day thinking, "I am the source of power for my life. I have to fix my problems. I have to be strong. I have to be god, since there isn't one." That's not only a scary thought, that's a depressing one. We need to know God in order to have hope from God.

Hope Breaker 2: When We Forget God

You'd think this one impossible until you remember the pattern of Israel in the Old Testament and our pattern still today. Forgetting God is a hope breaker because when it happens, we fail to remember the one who rescues us in times of trouble (Ps. 34:1–4). Pastor Mike Fabarez explains, "Forgetting God does not mean that we are unable to recall certain facts about God, but rather that he is no longer at the forefront of our minds and at the top of our priorities. Other things can so easily clutter our time and capture our attention until our worship, thanksgiving and dependence on God are all but an afterthought."[11]

Isn't it so easy to forget God? We go about our days that are filled with routine and ritual. In times of success, we grow comfortable in our own abilities and don't need God. As trouble abounds, we scramble to find solutions and we rely on our own ingenuity and strength to conquer challenges. Before we know it, waiting on God seems like a waste of time. Prayer becomes meaningless because it doesn't deliver immediate results. The Bible appears useless because reading it takes time away from solving our problems. Slowly but surely, like an engine gradually overheating, we make it some distance before boiling over and wondering how everything got to be so hopeless. When God is no longer our priority, our hope evaporates.

Hope Breaker 3: When We Feel Alone

Human beings, and specifically Christians, were created with a built-in need for community. Hope gets broken when relational bonds do or when feelings of loneliness push out the feeling of being loved. The word *community* gets thrown around a great deal in the church these days, so please resist the urge to think of potlucks and casseroles in an old multipurpose room at a Baptist church. I'm talking about real, genuine, authentic relationships in which people who love you tell the truth and walk with you, and you with them. The kind of relationships in which you can be who you are and that's good enough. The kind of relationships in which grace abounds and growth is allowed to take place slowly but surely. Too many people don't have this experience. They often feel like an Instagram highlight reel. You show your best. Look your best. And photoshop the rest. Meanwhile you're hopelessly dying inside.

Last year I was preparing to launch a special Q&A session for the students at our church. In the early planning stages, I was warned by a few volunteers that the students wouldn't ask anything. They had tried it in the past, and it did not have a lot of traction. But I didn't care, we were going to try it again. I told one of our interns to put two mic stands in each aisle and let students come up after the sermon. This brilliant eighteen-year-old normally would have just done what was asked, but in this case he wisely spoke up.

"Pastor Costi," he said, "it may be best to make it anonymous. I bet the students would ask more questions if they were spared the embarrassment of walking down an aisle and asking you something in front of so many peers. I could come up with a special QR code and put it on the screens. When students take a photo of that code with their phones, a form will pop up and they can ask anonymous questions that will go straight to a Google form on my phone, and I will ask you the random questions."

We went with his approach (how could we not?). The code went up on the screens during the first fifteen minutes of the service and right before the Q&A began. Numerous questions poured in. Hundreds, actually. And some of the most common ones went something like this: "I struggle with loneliness, depression, and suicidal thoughts. I just feel so hopeless."

In a church auditorium filled with people, with the Bible being taught, hugs and fist bumps overflowing, and worship abounding, *that* one-thousand-pound weight was crushing more than just a few students. In follow-up discussions with some of the ones who were struggling with loneliness, I found that most of them were sweet kids who got good grades and had stable home lives. Still, they felt hopeless because they felt alone. People are desperate for something more than just surface-level living. Loneliness can be such a killer—and not just spiritually.

Philip Zimbardo says, "I know of no more potent killer than isolation. There is no more destructive influence on physical and mental health than the isolation of you from me and of us from them. It has been shown to be a central agent in the etiology of depression, paranoia, schizophrenia, rape, suicide, mass murder, and a wide variety of disease states."[12] Loneliness crushes hope.

Hope Breaker 4: When We Don't See a Solution

Have you ever been in a situation in which you just didn't see a way out? When we get stuck in feelings of despair and see no escape, hopelessness—like claustrophobia—begins to press down on us until we can barely breathe. Fear will often do this to us. Fear tells us, "You can't conquer this. You aren't equipped to deal with this. There is no way out of this. You're defeated."

The inability to see a solution is one reason why people give up on life and commit suicide. More accurately stated, they see no solution to the problems they are facing but one—to end their life.

Hopelessness cannot be allowed to run wild and free. This hope breaker needs to be broken. We need help to see that there is always a solution. Suicide and other harmful acts are not it.

Hope Breaker 5: When We Struggle to See Our Purpose

One of my favorite recent movies is *The Call of the Wild.* It's a story about a dog named Buck and his unlikely relationship with a reclusive Yukon man named John Thornton. Buck is a cross-breed between a Saint Bernard and a Scotch shepherd and has always been a bit too big and rowdy for his fancy surroundings. After he is stolen and cast as a sled dog, a series of painful events enables him to slowly find his purpose. As for John Thornton, he is lost in despair—mourning the death of his son. The bottle has become his only solace. That and a map which supposedly leads to Yukon gold.

The movie is a powerful depiction of what purpose can do. It's also a sad reminder of how a lack of purpose can be a hope breaker. Throughout the movie we find John turning to alcohol to numb his pain, while Buck seems to never quite find a place to belong. Both characters wrestle with bouts of hopelessness linked to a lack of ultimate purpose. Eventually they are united and come to find a purpose together.

I think I love the movie so much because it relates to some of my own experiences. I think a lot of people feel that way about the movie. Perhaps you're like Buck. Without a clear purpose you're reckless, even if you're well-meaning. When you're not sure what your purpose is, you end up hopeless. Or perhaps you're like John Thornton. Pain, loss, and even your own mistakes have blinded you from your purpose. The equation is simple. No purpose equals no hope.

Five Hope Builders

You may need to take a deep breath after all that negative reflection. Those hope breakers are no joke. No wonder people experience hopelessness. But for the Christian, don't forget who gets the last word!

A man approached a Little League baseball game one afternoon. He asked a boy in the dugout what the score was. The boy responded, "Eighteen to nothing. We're behind."

"Boy," said the spectator, "I'll bet you're discouraged."

"Why should I be discouraged?" replied the little boy. "We haven't even gotten up to bat yet!"

Depending on where you're reading this, a nice loud, "Amen!" may be in order. It's time for the hope builders. Jesus is up to bat.

Hope Builder 1: Jesus Will Finish What He Has Started in You

I don't know about you, but I often forget about the heroes of the faith who are already in heaven, experiencing what we wait for with expectancy. We don't know for certain (theologically speaking) if our loved ones who are saved are watching and cheering us on, but we do know there are a cloud of witnesses already in heaven who see firsthand what Jesus can do. We also know that

Jesus promises to have the last word when it comes to our glorious future. That's a big deal because if what you're facing breeds hopelessness, remembering who you belong to and who is behind you will build hopefulness! The author of Hebrews will take it from here. I've added some emphasis to the phrases I want you to meditate on.

> Since we are surrounded by such a great cloud of witnesses, let us throw off everything that hinders and the sin that so easily entangles. And let us run with perseverance the race marked out for us, *fixing our eyes on Jesus, the pioneer and perfecter of faith.* For the joy set before him he endured the cross, scorning its shame, and sat down at the right hand of the throne of God. *Consider him who endured such opposition from sinners, so that you will not grow weary and lose heart.*
>
> —HEBREWS 12:1–3

The faith that saved Abraham and all of the other heroes of the faith listed in the book of Hebrews is the same faith that you can have in Jesus. You can endure this life not by your own strength but with his. This passage also has a key reminder about laying aside sins and weights that slow you down and keep you from experiencing greater joy in Jesus. Some people prefer to hold on to sins and weights like bitterness, unforgiveness, addictions, or even hatred, because these help us falsely justify our anger and hopelessness. They help us play the victim rather than the victor. Others struggle with hopelessness because their hope is attached to all the wrong things. When your hope is wrapped up in the things of this world and not in Jesus, you're bound to be disappointed.

A pastor friend of mine likens holding on to bitterness and

anger while trying to live the Christian life to running a marathon while wearing a parka. You may make it to the finish line, but you'll be overheated and will certainly double or triple the time it would've taken to reach your destination. You don't need to look to yourself for hope, and you don't need to hold on to playing the victim. You need to look to Jesus. He founded your faith. He finishes your faith. Best of all, he's seated at the right hand of God the Father and has big plans for your future. Focus on him so you don't grow weary and lose heart.

Hope Builder 2: Jesus Has Been Where You Are and Beat It

It would be one thing if Jesus were a detached deity who dwelt in some far-off, distant place. How unrelatable would that be? Even in the beginning of time, our God walked with his creation in some manner and form (Gen. 3:8). He is holy and set apart, yet he is still personal and relatable.

The author of Hebrews again delivers a hope builder, describing Jesus as one who has been where we are and can sympathize with us. Hebrews 4:14–16 declares, "Since we have a great high priest who has ascended into heaven, Jesus the Son of God, let us hold firmly to the faith we profess. For we do not have a high priest who is unable to empathize with our weaknesses, but we have one who has been tempted in every way, just as we are—yet he did not sin. Let us then approach God's throne of grace with confidence, so that we may receive mercy and find grace to help us in our time of need."

Jesus walked the road you're on and did it perfectly. If he's your Savior, you're going to make it—not because of you but in spite of you. Because of him, you aren't holding on to hope. Hope is holding on to you!

Hope Builder 3: Jesus Hasn't Left You Alone

One of the greatest fears that Jesus' disciples had was the same fear many people struggle with today. We think, "I don't want to be alone." His promise to them is still a promise for us: "I will not leave you as orphans; I will come to you" (John 14:18). These words that foreshadow his glorious return sit between a promise for the coming of the Holy Spirit and a promise that Jesus is in them and they are in him. All in all, those who have Jesus are never alone. When loneliness rears its ugly head, the believer can put it right back in its place by remembering the promises Jesus made. If this doesn't work, you may need to look more deeply at what you depend on.

I want to challenge you to assess your heart when it comes to dependency on people. As a people person, I am with you on the importance of relationships, friendships, and leaning on trustworthy people. At the same time, I believe we can depend on people too much and put time with others ahead of time with Jesus. When loneliness hits us, an overdependent person thinks, "I just need to be with people," before they think, "I just need to be with Jesus." Let me reiterate: we were made for relationships and need to lean on people. However, loneliness will persist when our dependence is on others and not on Jesus. If you are a believer, you are never alone. You may feel lonely, but Jesus is only a whisper away. You can talk to him, share your heart with him, and put your hope in him. Go to him first. He is there.

Hope Builder 4: Jesus Hears Your Prayers and Is Praying for You

Out of all five hope builders, this might be the one you think of the least but should remember the most. Have you ever prayed a prayer and wondered if Jesus is listening? Perhaps you've echoed the words of Psalm 130:1–2: "Out of the depths I cry to you, LORD; Lord, hear my voice. Let your ears be attentive to my cry for mercy." That is some serious expression about a serious need. But what usually comes next? Thoughts that go something like, "Jesus isn't listening. You're just talking into thin air. How silly and embarrassing to speak when no one is even there. With so many people praying at once, your prayers aren't important to God."

You know where lies like that come from? Only the devil himself talks like that (John 8:44). His goal is to blind you from ever fully seeing and appreciating this hope builder. Jesus hears your prayers and is praying for you. Look at these facts from the Bible:

- You can cast all your anxieties on God because he cares for you (1 Peter 5:7).
- God will unload wisdom onto you if you ask him and believe (James 1:5–8).
- God listens to those who worship and obey him (John 9:31).
- When you ask for things in line with his will, he hears you and will do it (1 John 5:14).
- The Lord hears the prayers of the righteous (1 Peter 3:12).

That settles that. Jesus hears your prayers. But is he really praying for you? Absolutely.

Romans 8:31 powerfully declares, "If God is for us, who can be against us?" and then assures us that Jesus Christ "is at the right hand of God and is also interceding for us" (v. 34). Hope is built up when we realize that Satan is a liar who constantly accuses people before God (Rev. 12:10), while Jesus is a mighty king who hears our prayers and is praying for us. Tune out the devil's lies. Tune in to Christ through prayer.

Hope Builder 5: Jesus Promises That Your Pain Will Have Purpose

One of the questions we tend to ask when enduring a painful experience is, what is this all for? Even if we have a high tolerance for painful trials, we usually have a low tolerance for not knowing the reason for them. The Bible repeatedly tells us that our pain and trials are going to have purposeful results. James 1:2–3 says that the testing of our faith will produce endurance. Who doesn't want more endurance for this life? Pain and trials are one way in which Jesus accomplishes that process. As with an athlete, the way to grow your endurance is to stretch your limits and push yourself beyond where you've been. Slowly but surely you will become one who endures.

Romans 5:3–5 also shows us the purpose in pain. Paul explains that suffering builds up our character, and that process creates hope. The cross of Jesus Christ is the greatest example of this hope builder. Through the cross, Jesus endured much pain, but none of it was pointless. No pain ever is. God will use it powerfully.

Is your hope built on Jesus? Trust him to turn your pain into purpose.

Questions for Reflection

1. List a few truths from this chapter that encouraged and/or challenged you.

2. Out of all the hope breakers, which one(s) hit home for you? Why?
3. Out of all the hope builders, which one(s) encouraged you? Why?
4. How is forgetfulness linked to hopelessness? How do you combat forgetfulness?
5. Loneliness can be a major factor in contributing to hopelessness. Is there someone you can encourage this week by spending more time with him or her?

CHAPTER 5

HE IS COMFORT

Praise be to the God and Father of our Lord Jesus Christ, the Father of compassion and the God of all comfort, who comforts us in all our troubles, so that we can comfort those in any trouble with the comfort we ourselves receive from God.

—2 CORINTHIANS 1:3-4

It happens on a Friday or Sunday night—after a long, hard week. Or when a weekday is especially grim. Comfort food calls my name. After spending some time with my wife, I wait for her to call it a night. She'll only ruin the fun by trying to deter me from my flavorful overload of sodium. It's only a matter of time before she turns and says, "I'm exhausted, honey. I'm going to head up to bed." That's my cue. For me, there's a specific list of culprits, and they are all chips. First, salt and malt vinegar chips. Second, dill pickle chips. Third, all-dressed chips ("#1 Flavor in Canada"). Fourth, nachos. I don't do all four in one night, but one of those usually makes an appearance. Though quite lightheartedly, my wife and I catch each other's eyes in the morning when she sees the bag in the trash or on the counter. If I beat her to the kitchen, the evidence of my chip binge is the first thing I try to hide. Somehow my sin always finds me out!

This scenario doesn't play out much these days, perhaps because we are too exhausted from wrangling our four kiddos (our fourth baby, Ruth Joy, was born in April of 2020 during the initial wave of COVID-19 lockdowns). Still, every so often my favorite comfort foods start calling my name again. Promising the soothing balm of comfort, potato chips deliver little more than a greasy aftermath and tighter pants.

Now, perhaps this isn't so bad. Are Christians not allowed to enjoy fun snacks? Of course we are. But how often can certain things—food, shopping, or sports—grab hold of our hearts and our habits? Pretty soon we find ourselves seeking to satisfy a spiritual need with physical pleasures. Like you, I know that I am supposed to go to Jesus first, but the temptation to self-medicate with instant gratification is always waiting nearby.

I recently took to Twitter and Instagram to poll followers about this chapter. There is a snapshot from the original tweet on the following page.

Hundreds responded on Instagram, and thousands of honest responses poured in on Twitter, including private messages from people asking for prayer regarding deeper struggles than the ones listed in the tweet. It clearly struck a nerve as so many people discovered that we all wrestle with finding comforts in pursuits

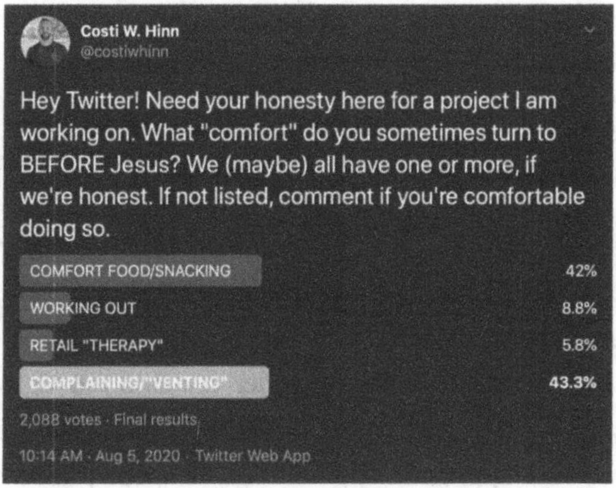
Costi W. Hinn
@costiwhinn
Hey Twitter! Need your honesty here for a project I am working on. What "comfort" do you sometimes turn to BEFORE Jesus? We (maybe) all have one or more, if we're honest. If not listed, comment if you're comfortable doing so.
COMFORT FOOD/SNACKING
42%
WORKING OUT
8.8%
RETAIL "THERAPY"
5.8%
COMPLAINING/"VENTING"
43.3%
2,088 votes · Final results
10:14 AM · Aug 5, 2020 · Twitter Web App

other than Christ. More than 85 percent of people sometimes turn to comfort food (as I do), or complaining and venting, before turning to Christ. Like many have said, "If you can't say amen, you can at least say ouch."

If we're human, we will at times turn to superficial comforts that are not Christ. And if we're honest, we'll admit that those comforts don't ever achieve the results we're chasing. They are really just thieves, stealing our comfort and leaving us high and dry. We could even go farther and say that they can easily turn into addictions that chain us to their appeal while only leaving us in greater bondage.

Whatever you're going through, determine to find your comfort in Christ. Shun the thief of false comfort. Your default habits and weaknesses do not have to own you. You may feel like you can't overcome them, but you must remember that the gospel doesn't just save you, it will transform you. God is not done with you, and he always finishes what he starts (Phil. 1:6).

But where do *you* start? I'm glad you asked. Start right where you are and begin to prioritize your comfort around the following three key ideas.

Three Keys to Christ-Centered Comfort

1. Turn to Jesus First

We know this scene (or some version of it) all too well, don't we? You wake up, reach for the phone, and a series of clicks and checks begins. In whatever order you find most pleasing: Facebook, Twitter, Instagram, email, text messages, weather app, workflow app, news app, TikTok, Snapchat, WhatsApp. Then, as the dopamine from all those notifications hits your system, you begin to feel a little guilty because you didn't even open your Bible app. So you do that—briefly—and the morning rush begins.

I was sitting with a mentor a few years ago, sharing honestly about feelings of anxiety, chaos, and being overwhelmed. For the most part, marriage, ministry, and life were blissfully sweet. But inside I felt a lack of comfort where it counted most. My spiritual life felt somewhat empty, and I felt like I was being pulled in every direction possible.

Suddenly he asked me what seemed to be an unrelated question. "What is your morning routine?"

Puzzled, I replied, "I wake up, brush my teeth, read my Bible, pray, have coffee, chat with my wife, and get ready for work."

He pressed in farther, asking, "What is your *exact* routine? As in, give me the second-by-second, move-by-move description of what you do."

I didn't quite know what he was getting at, but I decided to be as precise as possible. I said, "I wake up, check email to see what the day will look like, and click on a news app, then a social media app or two while I make my coffee. I may respond to an email that is important, write people back on social media, or send a text message or two. Then I sit at the kitchen table for quiet time."

His response was immediate. "Martin Luther once said, 'I have so much to do today, I'll need to pray for three hours just to get it all done.'"

The first shot of conviction hit my soul.

He continued. "What makes you think you'll do all that is required of you effectively, and have a clear mind, if the first thing on your mind is your task list, the endless drama of the news cycle, and the black hole of social media?"

The second shot of conviction hit my soul.

Again he continued. "If you want to experience the comfort of God, you need to prioritize the God of comfort. Before anything else, give yourself to him in prayer. And I mean *before* anything else."

The third shot of conviction hit my soul. Everything in me wanted to shout, "Legalism!" but I knew that was just my flesh reacting to the fact that I had been exposed. Why was I not experiencing comfort? Why was clarity becoming elusive? Why was I all over the map with spiritual busyness but had little spiritual vitality to show for it? I wasn't turning to Jesus first.

It may seem backward to most of us productivity junkies, but the best way to be productive is to pray. The best way to find comfort is not to itemize your MITs (most important tasks) with human strategies but rather to turn to Christ. It took only one day, and I was hooked. I'll never forget the first time I rolled out of bed and my arm felt like it was being magnetically drawn to my phone. Of course that was just my bad habit. Before long, prayer was becoming oxygen, and comfort was pouring into my soul.

For me, turning to Christ first was about praying before anything—literally anything—each morning. What is it for you? Perhaps it's asking Christ for wisdom before looking to your own solutions or intellect. Perhaps it's checking in with him before checking your bank account, counting your affirmations, or adding up your social media hits. Whatever it is, I want to lovingly extend the same challenge to you that my mentor offered me: "If you want to experience the comfort of God, you need to prioritize the God of comfort. Before anything else, give yourself to him in prayer. And I mean *before* anything else." Jesus is comfort.

2. Turn Off Complaining

I once presided over a funeral service for a man whose favorite line was, "If you're having negative thoughts, change your mind!" Isn't that a great reminder? One of the best ways to send your mind crashing into negativity is by complaining. Complaining is a comfort thief. It is rooted in a lack of gratitude and in discontentment toward God. Complaining shifts the blame for our unhappiness onto other people and onto God. Complaining feeds off pride that beckons us, "Tell the world how you feel! It will change things." But if we're honest, complaining deflates things. It deflates others. It deflates joy. It deflates morale. It deflates positivity. It deflates optimism. It deflates hope. It deflates growth. It deflates thanksgiving. But worst of all, it deflates your witness.

Paul wrote the letter of Philippians to a group of people who had plenty to complain about. They were not very popular, and most of their friends and family were loyal citizens of Rome and hardly sympathetic to Christians. The believers in Philippi were not living the dream. Most shocking of all, Paul was in chains when he wrote this letter, yet its central theme is joy. Yes, joy. The chained apostle wrote to vulnerable Christians in a culture that despised them, and he spoke about joy! In Philippians 2:14–16, he had the audacity to say, "Do everything without grumbling or arguing, so that you may become blameless and pure, 'children of God without fault in a warped and crooked generation.' Then you will shine among them like stars in the sky as you hold firmly to the word of life. And then I will be able to boast on the day of Christ that I did not run or labor in vain." Did Paul validate complaining? Did he say, "Go ahead and vent. It's good for the soul"? Not at all. Paul's words to the Christians in Philippi drove home not just the what but also the why. It's obvious that we are not to complain, but the reason is because we have an opportunity to be a witness.

The world's default settings are set to "complain." Most unbelievers make venting a sport. They fire off about however they feel, trash-talk the boss, and spew out whatever else they are unhappy about. Have you ever been that person or sat with someone who is? Do you feel better afterward or worse? Are your problems solved or still looming? Is comfort closer or farther?

Being a Christian doesn't mean we are immune to complaining, but it does mean we have a solution to it. We will find comfort in Christ much more quickly if we cease complaining. As with a circuit breaker on the side of your house, cut the power to it altogether and it will cease to function. I want to challenge you to treat complaining like a circuit breaker that has to be shut off. Kill the power to it. Renew your mind (Rom. 12:2) and choose to see complaining for what it is. Ask the Holy Spirit to help you bear fruit (Gal. 5:22–23), and invite your spouse, family, and friends to keep you accountable. That is where the third key comes in.

3. Turn to Trusted Sources

Using this key to comfort starts with embracing the hard truth of Proverbs 27:6, which says, "Wounds from a friend can be trusted, but an enemy multiplies kisses." The people who love us don't tell us what we want to hear, they tell us what we need to hear. If we're going to rethink our source of comfort, we need to rethink our social connections. Realizing that God uses people to speak truth into our lives, we must keep the vital truth of this proverb in mind.

We know God speaks to us through the Bible. We believe he speaks to us through the preaching in church, when it is done faithfully. And we may feel he speaks to us through biblical teaching in books, blogs, and videos. But how often do we think of God using the people around us to speak to us? People are vessels for his use (2 Tim. 2:20–21), and the Bible describes how God uses them to declare truth (Rom. 10:14–17; 1 Thess. 2; 1 Peter 4:7–11). While nobody is speaking new revelation on the same level as Scripture, God is still using people today in our lives to deliver his truth, in line with Scripture. So the question becomes all the more important: who is speaking into your life, and what are they speaking?

Turn to trusted sources when you are sharing your hurts, struggles, and pains. If you're lost and confused, you must be careful not to invite the wrong kind of wisdom into your life. Do the people you turn to in times of need encourage you or drain you? Do they point you to Jesus or point at your problems? Are they planting seeds of doubt or planting seeds of gospel truth?

When they leave your presence, is there an aroma of hope or a feeling of despair? Chronic complainers will kill your comfort. Christ-exalting encouragers will ignite it. God uses people in powerful ways to bring truth into our lives. Make sure the ones you trust, trust in him too.

The War against Your Comfort

The three keys outlined in the previous section are biblical and bound to work if put into practice regularly. There's just one problem: your efforts to employ them are not going to go unnoticed. The devil is highly invested in your seeking comfort outside of Christ. His primary goal is to steal, kill, and destroy (John 10:10). He works night and day against Jesus, and he likes to work in underhanded ways so as not to be noticed.

There are two weapons Satan employs to attack your Christ-centered comfort: discontent and comparison.

Weapon 1: Discontent

If our adversary can pollute our contentment in Christ, he can pull us off the pathway of comfort that God has purposed for us. Contentment is a priceless treasure of Christian character. The devil knows this, so he goes after it. But contentment can be a challenge not only because of his attacks on it but also because you're not born with it. No one is born with contentment already mastered. It is not natural. It is learned over time. But as with all things that must be learned, if you'll commit to practicing it, eventually it can become a habit. Sound impossible? With Jesus it is not.

Philippians 4:13 makes one of the most famous statements in

all the Bible. You'll find it quoted by famous athletes and appearing on billboards, T-shirts, social media posts, and tattoos. Paul writes, "I can do all things through him who strengthens me" (ESV). We tend to hear that and associate it with winning a game, making it through a rough day, or nailing a job interview. However, when Paul makes this statement, he is not referring to hitting a game-winning shot or landing a dream job. The context of his statement is finding strength in God no matter what the circumstances are. "I have learned to be content whatever the circumstances. I know what it is to be in need, and I know what it is to have plenty. I have learned the secret of being content in any and every situation, whether well fed or hungry, whether living in plenty or in want. I can do all this through him who gives me strength" (Phil. 4:11–13).

You can find lasting comfort if your contentment is wrapped up in Christ. You do not have to end up wallowing in despair, no matter what you're facing. Through Jesus you can do all things, including the seemingly impossible task of being content with any circumstance in life.

To take this even farther, you can actually rejoice in all your circumstances. In 1 Thessalonians 5:16–18, Paul encourages our attitude and our actions, saying, "Rejoice always, pray continually, give thanks in all circumstances; for this is God's will for you in Christ Jesus." If there were a perfect summary statement for this chapter, it would be this passage. God's will is not as hard to see as we sometimes make it out to be. He wants us to be a people who rejoice, who pray, and who give thanks to him no matter what. Think of contentment as a vehicle, and thanksgiving as the fuel. Put them both together, and you'll be well on your way to your God-ordained destination: Christ-centered comfort.

Weapon 2: Comparison

The second weapon the enemy uses to assault us is comparison. This is one of Satan's go-to weapons because comparison is the thief of joy. He sends comparison every day from the pit of hell directly to the doorstep of your heart. It's one of Satan's oldest weapons and is aimed at upending your Christ-centered comfort. The devil wants you to become uncomfortable with an eternal strategy and seek out an earthly and material one. Comparison enters our minds and comes out of our mouths with statements like:

- I wish I had her looks.
- I wish I had his job.
- Why do they always get what they want?
- If I had that, I would be happy too.
- How come God made life so hard for me?
- What makes them so special?
- I wish my husband did that for me.
- If only my wife acted more like she does.
- Why can't my kids be like theirs?
- I wish I had that house.

And on and on and on we could go. Do you notice what comparison includes a whole lot of? Me, my, I, wish, if, why, and them. When our eyes are locked in on comparison with others, they cannot be on Christ. If he is where we find comfort, how can we expect to find it by looking over the fence and into the life of our neighbor? Keep a close eye on comparison in seasons when you are experiencing trials. In times of weakness, Satan is merciless. Where jealousy and selfish ambition are, every evil work abounds (James 3:16). Where evil work resides, you will usually find comparison lurking somewhere nearby. When turning to Christ first, be sure to confess comparison and place it at the foot of the cross. Once you do, your hands will be free to receive the kind of comfort only Jesus provides.

Jesus Can Use You to Bring Comfort

It would be terribly wrong to assume that someone enduring pain is not able to minister to someone else as a vessel through which God brings comfort to others. God's blessings can most certainly come through like-minded friends who can relate to our pain because they're feeling it too. What's more? Nearly all of the Bible's great heroes and heroines suffered to some degree. Their comfort was truly wrapped up in Christ.

Even though suffering is like a school you're never excited to graduate from, the degree you earn opens doors and opportunities that can make you grateful—yes, grateful—for whatever you've endured. But sometimes it's difficult to see how you can be useful as a suffering Christian. If that's you, remember that through suffering, God has given you a unique vantage point from which you can encourage someone else. He's also given you the opportunity to showcase faithfulness in the midst of the fire, and perspective in the midst of pain. In many ways, when you glorify God no matter what you're going through, you are living proof of Jesus' words to his disciples in Matthew 5:14–16: "You are the light of the world. A town built on a hill cannot be hidden. Neither do people light a lamp and put it under a bowl. Instead they put it on its stand, and it gives light to everyone in the house. In the same way, let your light shine before others, that they may see your good deeds and glorify your Father in heaven." Your suffering is an opportunity to shine for Jesus. That can bring great comfort to others.

The church is supposed to be the place where you find the endless blessing of comforting friends, but you do not have to be a longtime church member to know that sometimes the church can be deficient in this area. Though other reasons could be mentioned, I believe that one surpasses them all: ignorance. Many people in the church, contrary to popular belief, do not know what to say or how to say it.

My hope is that the rest of this chapter serves all of us as we try to be an extension of Jesus. He *is* comfort, and he uses his people to be ministers of his comfort.

Hockey Friends with Broken Hearts

I'll never forget meeting Mark. Our common ground went beyond our faith in Christ: we both had ice running through our veins. Hockey ice, that is. When I first met Mark, I was a Canadian-bred, hockey-loving pastor who was serving in Southern California. He was a Michigan-bred, hockey-loving man. Both Mark and his wife, Chelsea, were as passionate about Jesus as I was, and as crazy about hockey too. If their favorite team (the Detroit Red Wings) beat my favorite team (the Toronto Maple Leafs) on a Saturday night, Chelsea would go out of her way to let me know about it on Sunday morning before the worship service started. Their friendship within the church became a fun and refreshing gift from the Lord in so many ways, which is why my wife and I couldn't contain our excitement and joy when they announced they were pregnant. We knew just the gift we'd get to welcome little baby Joselyn Grace into the world.

We customized the jersey (their favorite team's, not ours) with her name on the back, and my wife added rhinestones one by one around the jersey number. "It has to be girly," she insisted. We wrapped it, boxed it, and it was ready to go. Then the news came.

Baby Joselyn would never get to wear her jersey. The Master had called her home. In Mark and Chelsea's own words, here's what happened.

> From the very beginning, our pregnancy journey was a difficult one. The hardest season began in the second trimester when we discovered our daughter had multiple abnormalities. Every doctor's appointment seemed to include a new abnormality to add to the list as her prognosis worsened. The doctors suggested termination as her life expectancy was grim. At one point, we were given a 2 percent life expectancy for our sweet girl and faced potential health risks for Chelsea if we wanted to continue carrying our daughter. We clung to God's Word, standing firm in our belief that God ordains the length of each life. Termination was not an option, regardless of a prognosis, no matter how difficult or traumatic the circumstances were. We believe that God is always sovereign and in control, and that if he has willed such pain and hardship in our lives, then he would grow us and sustain us through every moment. That is exactly what we experienced.
>
> During the traumatic thirty-eight weeks of pregnancy, God sustained us. Through the ups and downs of crippling morning sickness, through countless doctors' appointments, hospital visits, and monitoring sessions. It was the absolute best and the absolute worst thirty-eight weeks of our lives. To be in such despair, and yet have so much joy. To feel so

weak, and yet watch our faith and marriage be strengthened. To be consumed with all the "what ifs" and worries, and then to be able to turn to the Bible and renew our minds with his truth brought such joy, peace, and understanding. It was so painfully beautiful. And still is. We'd be lying if we said our hearts aren't broken. Every time we see other parents enjoying their children, it is a stinging reminder of our sweet Joselyn. It is so very hard to express our pain, especially to friends who may not understand that our grieving process takes time, sometimes much longer than we had even expected. We know what the Bible says, and that brings us such hope and peace, but sometimes it takes a little longer than we'd like for the message to mend our broken hearts. "But God." Those two words have become the life raft we cling to when the waters of pain are so deep we cannot swim. His grace is sufficient in our greatest times of weakness. That is a promise we hold on to each day.

The Russian Roulette of Christian Response

When people in our lives go through this sort of pain, the response from Christians can be like a game of Russian roulette: you just never know what you're going to get. Some of us aren't sure what to say, so we say nothing. Others are scared to say the wrong thing, so they don't say anything either. Still others try to say the right thing but end up doing more harm than good. But there is even another group—those who, for any number of reasons, are selfishly indifferent to the pain that others are experiencing. We all may fit into this last group from time to time, no matter how much we don't want to admit it.

Like an archer painting a bull's-eye around where his arrow hits, we tend to act like we know what we're talking about when, in reality, far too many of us are unable to construct our responses on a foundation of biblical understanding. We are left wondering what it means to come alongside those who are experiencing great loss. Exactly how do we do it?

In light of our great need to be ambassadors for Jesus and bring comfort to those in great pain, there are at least four responses we can all prioritize.

1. Show Empathy toward Them

Empathy and sensitivity are not weaknesses—as some might think. Some of us may struggle with being sensitive to others, but through Christ we can all exhibit such care. Paul's words in Romans 12:15 instruct the church on how to serve one another: "Rejoice with those who rejoice; mourn with those who mourn." In the most basic sense, it is a downright Christian behavior to show emotion that is appropriate for the moment. Feelings matter, and empathy is one of those feelings that Christians should cultivate for the good of those around them. We serve a compassionate God (James 5:11), we have a Savior who wept over a loss (John 11:35), and the one who holds the world in his hands holds our tears in a bottle (Ps. 56:8 ESV). Emotions are not bad, they're a tool for bonding. It may take some effort, but you are called to show empathy to those who are mourning.

2. Listen to Them

We can all do a better job at this one. Parents who have lost their babies, people struggling with the loss of a spouse, individuals navigating difficult illness—most of them want to talk about it. They *need* to talk about it. We do well to put aside our emotional toolboxes and listen. These people don't need fixing.

One of the most awe-inspiring examples of listening in the Bible doesn't even involve talking. A godly man named Job (more on him later) suffered an excruciating trial, losing his cattle, sheep, camels, servants, and—worst of all—his sons and daughters, all in one day. Word spread of the terrible tragedy. Job 2:11–13 says, "When Job's three friends . . . heard about all the troubles that had come upon him, they set out from their homes and met together by agreement to go and sympathize with him and comfort him. When they saw him from a distance, they could hardly recognize him; they began to weep aloud, and they tore their robes and sprinkled dust on their heads. Then they sat on the ground with him for seven days and seven nights. No one said a word to him, because they saw how great his suffering was." Job's friends "listened" to the pain of their friend by simply saying nothing.

Want to be a listening ear? Sit silently and hear the pain of those around you. Sometimes we comfort those around us best when we have the courage to just sit with them in their pain.

3. Serve Them

In his book *Comfort the Grieving*, Paul Tautges charts bereavement plans that last up to three years. How's that for serving? Though not everyone will be able to hold down the fort for a three-year plan, the idea is to serve those who are in pain. Jesus served to the point of laying down his life (Matt. 20:28). He was the ultimate example of selflessness and humility (Phil. 2:3–7), and we are to be devoted to one another with the same attitude of service (Rom. 12:9–13). That requires a good look in the mirror. Does ignorance, indifference, selfishness (whether we know it or not), compassion fatigue, or your own trials keep you from serving others? Are your idols or busyness barricading your heart from being able to show more love to others?

Maybe it's time to say to someone who's grieving, "What do you want? Consider it done." "What do you need? I'll do it right now." "Please inconvenience me. I am here for you."

4. Journey with Them

Reminding people about the sovereignty of God is a great thing. Telling people to "consider it pure joy" when they encounter trials (James 1:2) is also a great thing. But rapidly discharged sentiments, no matter how biblical, have little impact without ongoing relationship. We need to inconvenience ourselves, crush our selfishness, and make the effort to forge relationships. Every ounce of "me" must be squeezed out of our sinful hearts if we want to walk with someone the way Christ intends us to.

Relationship opens the door for trust, and trust enables us to say the things we need to say to one another. Speaking the truth in love is possible all the time, but it is especially effective when we do so with people with whom we share a deep and trusting relationship. Drive-by one-liners like, "Stay focused on eternity. You'll see your baby in heaven one day," or, "Keep your perspective during this time. Millions of people die every day" are useless maxims when the pain of loss is searing someone's heart. Journeying with people enables us to spend time with them and opens the door for us to share wisdom, encouragement, and even correction. Remember, you can be someone's trusted source of Christ-centered comfort by using your relationship with that person to point to Jesus.

We Need Each Other

Notice what mourning with those who mourn is not about? Yep, you guessed it! It's not about you. Your opinion on timelines, perspective, or even well-intentioned sharing of how you conquered previous pain is not essential to this process. It is Christ who provides the best recipe for restoring the broken heart. Selflessness is the mark of Christlikeness, and there is no better way to be the church to those around you than to emulate the life Jesus modeled for us.

Your moment will come too. Pain is a reality that we are all going to experience. Taking practical steps enables us all to bear one another's burdens and be the hands and feet of Christ.

Questions for Reflection

1. List a few truths from this chapter that encouraged and/or challenged you.
2. Which do you struggle with the most: contentment or comparison? Why?
3. Why is it vital for people who are sick, suffering, and hurting to remember that they can be useful, powerful vessels in God's hand? Have you ever experienced encouragement and inspiration from a suffering Christian's perspective?

4. List three or four distractions that regularly hinder your prayer life. What steps can you take to immediately prioritize uninterrupted prayer each day?
5. What can you do to support your church or local community by bringing comfort to those around you who are hurting? Read 1 John 3:17–18 and commit to putting this into action.

CHAPTER 6

HE IS GOOD

> *Taste and see that the* L*ORD is good;*
> *blessed is the one who takes refuge in him.*
>
> —PSALM 34:8

You say it, I say it, we all say it.

It usually comes out when we purchase our first home, deliver a healthy baby, find a perfect front row parking spot at the grocery store, hit the road for summer vacation, or get promoted at work. "God is so good!"

There couldn't be a more reassuring truth. He most certainly is good. We say it because it is one of the best ways to express our appreciation to God for how things are working out in our favor and for giving us a temporary state of happiness and excitement. Would we say the same thing, however, if things were not working out the way we desired? Do we truly embrace the fact that

God is good, even when our circumstances are not? Could there be more to his goodness than just the bright side of our story? If we're going to grow closer to Jesus than ever before and find our ultimate purpose in who he is (and not merely in what he can do), we must ask ourselves these kinds of challenging questions. They are essential to our growth.

God Is Good All the Time

When things are going right, we rightly declare God's goodness, but the Bible clearly shows us that God is still good when things are going horribly wrong. This is because goodness is part of God's nature. He is always good, because it is innate to who he is.

God allowed Satan to afflict Job with suffering as part of a test (Job 1:6–12). Even still, God is good. Paul begged the Lord to remove a "thorn in the flesh," but God did not (2 Cor. 12:7–10). He is still good. When King Nebuchadnezzar commanded Shadrach, Meshach, and Abednego to bow down and worship the idol he'd raised, they refused. The king threatened to have them thrown into a fiery furnace. Their response? They declared that their God was able to deliver them, but even if he didn't, they would not worship any other gods (Dan. 3:17–18). Those men knew that God is good, even if he didn't deliver them from a blazing death.

Now personalize this truth. Is God still good if you lose your job, if you lose your home, if you can't have a child, or if a doctor says you have six months to live? Answering that question will test your view of God. God's goodness is based on his character. Which means that your career advancement and good health are unrelated to whether he is good. He *is* good and he is good *all the time*, no matter what our circumstances might be.

The Biblical Reality of God's Goodness

Scripture is not silent on this subject. Countless passages point to the goodness of God throughout the ups and downs of life. For example, the apostle John wanted to shape and protect the way Christians viewed God, as do I. So when false teachers misrepresented the gospel, he reminded believers, "This is the message we have heard from him and declare to you: God is light; in him there is no darkness at all" (1 John 1:5). Regarding John's writing style, Charles Spurgeon said, "The apostle John's style was to give you a truth then guard that truth." In this case, John's statement that "God is light" is doubled down with the declaration that "in him there is no darkness at all." What John is saying here can be paraphrased this way: "In case you were wondering if God isn't *all* light, or if maybe some element of him can sin, that's not possible. If you somehow think that his anger, wrath, sovereignty, and judgments are his dark side, and his goodness, love, joy, mercy, and grace are his light side, that's not possible. He is all light and *always* light."

God isn't like some of today's movie superheroes, complete with a troubling dark side that must be hidden or tamed. Every aspect of who he is and what he does is good. This truth impacts how we view him in our darkest moments, because we can still know that he is light. He is good. We don't need to cry out in anguish, wondering if he still has a handle on things or if he has suddenly turned into a monster. Such a thing will never be. God is good.

Discussion about God's goodness in the midst of horrible situations in our world begs the question, why did God create evil? But that question contains a false assumption. Nowhere in the Bible are we taught that God created evil, has evil in him, or is the author of evil. We know from the Bible that God can cause calamity and bad events to occur, and therefore, certainly allow it (Lam. 3:38; Amos 3:6; Isa. 45:7), but since there is no evil in him, we can trust that his purposes and judgments are still ultimately for good. Someday, we know, he will eradicate evil. Since God cannot eradicate himself, we can fully affirm that he is not at all evil. Instead he will judge all evil one day.

Most helpful of all for your immediate situation is that God can take something evil and make it work out for good. That is a truth we need to keep close to our hearts.

God Works All Things for Good

Romans 8:28 is a very important passage to address when we're talking about the goodness of God in all circumstances. Paul writes, "We know that for those who love God all things work together for good, for those who are called according to his purpose" (ESV). Often you may hear a person or a preacher say that this passage means that everything happening to you is going to turn out for your good, that the blessing is just on the other side of this burden, that your prosperity is going to come from the pain. Basically, this approach to Romans 8:28 sees good as *your* definition of good. This is not the right way to handle this passage.

No matter how well intentioned, another inappropriate handling of Romans 8:28 is to throw it around after a tragedy as though it makes everything fine. Does it have a place in the wake of painful events? Yes. But most of the time, it's needed only after the initial mourning process slowly begins to give space for reflection and deeper conversation. How many of us know that in the early stages of pain, we just need prayer and for others to mourn with us, not statements (no matter how true) about how it's all going to be okay? There are many tragedies that will never be okay. We simply learn to lean on Jesus, grateful that he is holding on to us.

So what does Romans 8:28 mean, and how does understanding it fit into our growing closer to Jesus? First, it is speaking specifically about "those who love God," "those who are called according to his purpose." Those phrases are directly aimed at believers, which means this is not a general promise you can throw around at people, like a prosperity gospel preacher telling a crowd that God will make them happy, healthy, and wealthy. Second, this passage says "all things," which means that the good, the bad, and the ugly *will* happen. No one is immune to the "all things" in life. Third, this passage reminds us that God's definition of good is what will ultimately be accomplished, and his good will be good for us. One of my favorite explanations of this passage is by Randy Alcorn.

> The focus is not on isolated events in the believer's life, but on the sum total of all events. Do you see the difference between saying "each thing by itself is good" and "all things work together for good"? Think about it. The difference is tremendous. The verse does not tell me I should say "it is good" if my leg gets broken, or my house burns down, or I am robbed and beaten, or my child dies. But it does say that God will use these events and weave them together with every other facet of my life in order to produce what He knows to be the very best for me. . . . Once I heard a pastor say, "I'm tired of hearing

> people tritely use Romans 8:28." So am I. But I am *not* tired of Romans 8:28 itself and pray that I never will be. When you use this powerfully explosive verse (and you should use it), handle it with care. But whatever you do, don't stay away from it. The truth it contains can change your whole outlook on life.[13]

In light of the great truth contained in Romans 8:28, and all that the Bible teaches about the goodness of God, we do well to internalize at least three powerful truths that can transform our perspective in the midst of pain.

1. God Is the Giver of All Good Things

Our pride tells us that we are responsible for earning good things, good income, and even good results from hard work. That may be true to an extent, but it's not the whole story. While you are the one who goes to work each day to earn income, and you are the one who goes to the gym to improve your health, and you are the one who performs with excellence and gets a promotion, all of the good things in your life are from God. More than that, even the ability to work hard or do anything good is a gift given to you by God. James 1:17 reminds us, "Every good and perfect gift is from above, coming down from the Father of the heavenly lights, who does not change like shifting shadows."

When we see good things through this lens, entitlement shatters and gratitude soars. Entitlement emanates from a heart that believes it deserves everything it gets. Entitlement tells us, "You shouldn't be dealing with this right now. You're such a good person. You deserve so much more!" We silence entitlement by reminding ourselves that we are undeserving recipients of so many good things from God. Suddenly we can be in the middle of pain, cancer treatments, relational conflict, or an anxiety attack and still maintain a heart posture that overflows with thanksgiving toward the Giver of good.

2. God Is Good Even When Our Circumstances Are Not

All through the Bible, God's people encounter both immensely good times and horribly hard times. Yet through it all, the Bible declares God's goodness. The psalms are filled with declarations of God's goodness, made by David even when he is going through pain. Enduring King Saul's jealous rage and attempts to kill him (1 Sam. 18:11; 19:10), experiencing injustices and betrayals (1 Sam. 23:15–29), waiting years to take his rightful place as king, running like a fugitive from his own rebellious and tyrannical son (2 Sam. 15:13–17:22), David still declares the goodness of God. Psalm 106:1 exalts God, exclaiming, "Praise the LORD. Give thanks to the LORD, for he is good; his love endures forever." Psalm 107:1 repeats these words, and so does Psalm 118:1 and Psalm 136:1. The theme of thanksgiving is prevalent in these praises, which reminds us again that we can praise God in the midst of pain. He is good, even when our circumstances are not!

3. God Is Going to Turn Our Pain into Purpose

A pastor friend and his wife lost a baby boy several years ago and were enduring deep pain. The wife was particularly struggling with all of the jovial, well-intentioned platitudes offered by chipper people. Perhaps you've heard some version of these too.

- "It's going to be okay!"
- "God is up to something great, we just don't know what it is yet!"
- "God is going to turn your mourning into joy!"

She slowly began to turn callous toward encouragement from people because, like others who have lost a child, she understood that you never really recover. Those who had never lost a child just couldn't seem to get that a pithy statement did nothing to meet her in her pain. As with losing a limb, you never quite get used to the loss, you just learn to live with it. She was confused. She was hurting. She was misunderstood.

Then one day another pastor looked at this grieving couple and said something that finally made sense. He didn't promise that God was going to take away the pain. He didn't promise that they'd receive some big financial blessing for their burdens. He didn't promise that the situation was ever going to be okay. He simply said, "God does not necessarily take the pain away, but he will take that pain and turn it into purpose." Years later that couple still mourn the loss of their sweet boy, but God has used their pain to minister to other parents who have needed a shoulder to lean on through tragic loss and confusion. Do they have all the answers? No. But they have a renewed perspective and sense of purpose in the midst of pain.

In the following chart are several biblical examples of how suffering and trials are used by God and can result in good. These show that God's goodness means more than just our growth here on earth. His goodness reverberates beyond our lives, leading to goodness for those around us and generations beyond us, as well as an eternal reward in heaven.

THE PERSON	THE PAIN	THE PURPOSE
Jesus (Isa. 53; 2 Cor. 5:21; 1 Peter 2:24)	Jesus is beaten, mocked, tortured, denied, abandoned; he takes on sin for the sinner's sake; he is killed on a cross.	Present: Jesus pays the penalty of sin; God's wrath is satisfied. Future: Believers are given eternal life; there is hope for humanity.
Job (Job 1–3; 38–42)	Job loses his kids, his health, and his wealth; his wife says, "Curse God!"	Present: Job experiences a deeper relationship with God, is blessed by God, is restored. He refutes the arguments of his friends and proves he is not being punished for his sins. Future: Job shows us that trials are not always punishment for sin. He shows that we can endure terrible trials and still bless and worship God, and that by doing so, we prove our faith, defeat Satan, and vindicate God's goodness.
Paul (2 Cor. 12:7–10)	An unspecified "thorn in the flesh" plagues Paul. He prays to have it removed, but God won't alleviate his torment.	Present: Paul experiences the extravagance of God's grace and learns that God's power is perfected in weak people. He teaches this truth to the Corinthian church. Future: Believers learn to accept God's no and rely on his power when they are weak.
Elizabeth (Luke 1:5–45)	A righteous and faithful wife, Elizabeth endures the disgrace of infertility.	Present: In her old age, Elizabeth is shown the favor of the Lord and miraculously gives birth to John the Baptist; she supports Mary and shares the joy of her becoming the mother of the Messiah. Future: Elizabeth is a model of faithfulness and an example to all believers, as one of the first people to ever proclaim Jesus as her Lord.
Peter (Luke 22:31–34)	Satan asks permission to sift Peter like wheat—and is allowed. Peter denies Jesus and fails him.	Present: Peter is restored, becomes a pillar of strength in the early church. He suffers faithfully, never to deny his Lord again. Future: Peter shows believers that personal failure cannot separate them from the love and saving power of Jesus.

These examples are just the tip of the iceberg. When we search the pages of Scripture, we find that God is good no matter what we're going through, and that his purposes and methods go far beyond what we can comprehend, echoing into the community around us and down through generations after us. That doesn't change the reality of our pain at times, but as real as the suffering is, the rewards and blessings for those who remain faithful are monumentally greater.

Though God may allow Satan to roam the earth on a leash for a time, there is coming a day when Satan will be bound and cast into the lake of fire for all eternity (Rev. 20:1–15). In the grand scheme of things, he is simply a pawn on God's chessboard as the Lord works all things together to accomplish his good (Rom. 8:28).

Always remember, God's choice to allow your trials is rooted in love. He loves you so much that he will grow you and shape you until eternity, then reward you for being faithful. How good is that? Well, it certainly won't feel good all the time, but as you seek him in the midst of your pain, my prayer is that you will find a sense of supernatural joy as God uses trials to test you, shape you, and grow you for his glory (Phil. 1:6).

God is good . . . all the time.

Questions for Reflection

1. List a few truths from this chapter that encouraged and/or challenged you.
2. Write down one example of a time when you were experiencing a painful trial but could still see how God is good. Next, write down one example of a time when

you were experiencing great blessing and could see how God is good.

3. Read the following passages and jot down one clear truth from each about the goodness of God.
   Luke 18:19
   James 1:17
   Psalm 34:8
4. Why is it so important for Christians to evaluate God's goodness according to his character rather than their circumstances?
5. Who can you encourage with the truths you've learned or been reminded of in this chapter? Call, text, or email that person today.

CHAPTER 7

HE IS LOVE

> *Dear friends, since God so loved us, we also ought to love one another.*
>
> —1 JOHN 4:11

One of my favorite quotes about Christian pleasure and Christian pain is by C. S. Lewis, because it can be applied to God's love for us, even if our circumstances don't make us feel very loved.

He says, "God whispers to us in our pleasures, speaks in our conscience, but shouts in our pains: it is his megaphone to rouse a deaf world." I take this to mean that God does care about our pleasures, but they are not the primary way that he draws us closer to him or makes himself known. Our pleasures are also not the loudest way that God tells us how much he loves us. As in the truest friendship and the most committed marriage, we don't fully know unconditional love until we realize how much someone loves us in the bad times, not just the good. Of course, pleasures are how we experience God's goodness, but in times of pleasure we tend to forget God. We grow complacent. Comfortable. Forgetful. But suffering and trials tend to draw us closer to him. Pain leaves us nowhere to go but to our knees, and it is through pain that God shouts his reminder that he loves us, that his grace is sufficient for our weakness (2 Cor. 12:9), and that nothing can separate us from his love (Rom. 8:38–39). God uses suffering not only to increase your attention to him but also to increase your affection for him. Furthermore, God can use your affliction to show you his affection. He is the definition of love. He is the initiator of love. And he loves you. Period.

I was reading just this past week about a pastor named John Fawcett who, in 1773, was pastoring a small, poor church in Wainsgate, England, when a large and influential church in London called him to be their pastor. He was a powerful preacher and a gifted writer, and those talents opened the door for opportunity. But as the wagons were loaded with the Fawcett family belongings and the church members came to say their farewells, Mary Fawcett began to cry. She said boldly to her husband, "John, I cannot bear to leave!" He broke down as well and responded, "Nor can I. We shall remain here with our people." The wagons were unloaded, and John Fawcett spent his entire fifty-four-year ministry at Wainsgate with the people he loved so dearly. It was this experience that inspired him to write the beautiful hymn "Blest Be the Tie That Binds." This story reminds us that love is powerful. God uses love not only to show us the bond we share with him but also to demonstrate the bond we can have with others.

In this chapter, I first want to look briefly at how the world defines love, then look at how Jesus defines love, and then give us a road map for how to live out our love. No matter what you're going through, God will use the way you love others to transform the world around you. The question is, do we know what love is and what it isn't?

A Transactional Love

This world typically defines love as something that is *about you* and *feelings based*. Magazines and websites put endless amounts of time and money into marketing love to hopeful hearts and hopeless romantics. Articles may tout the "Ten Ways to Make Him Fall for You," or the "Seven Reasons She's Just Not into You." These magazines and online publications promise surefire ways to land the love you've always wanted and keep the flame of feelings burning bright. Love, it seems, is much more of a product or commodity than anything else. This approach turns matrimony into manipulation, friendship into transaction. Could it be that such worldly definitions of love permeate our hearts and minds? Is it possible that in our sinful and fallen flesh, we might even be attracted to this kind of transactional love because it makes love all about what we can get out of other people?

Jesus knows what your spirit needs: his love. It's not a transactional love, it's a transformational love. It's not based on feelings. It's based on facts.

A Transformational Love

What can we know about God and his transformational love? Let's look at four truths taught in the Bible.

1. God Is Love

Any real understanding of genuine love must begin with God's definition of love, because he *is* the definition of love. Like goodness, love is one of God's attributes. First John 4:7–8 says, "God is love" (literally "love is God" in the original Greek).

Furthermore, the love that God is, is an unconditional kind of love. This means that even in a world reeling with hate, even with odds stacked against you, even if you've experienced unimaginable hatred and betrayal, the most important love cannot be stopped by anything you or I ever do. If God loves you, he loves you without conditions!

Can I make an even bolder assertion? Even though there are many important kinds of relational loves to be experienced on planet Earth (such as marital, familial, or friendship), God's love is the only love that will matter in the end. The reality of God's love transcends earth and goes on into eternity. That he could love you, and that you could love him, is an exchange unlike any other.

The Bible teaches several key truths that help us better understand God's love. To grow closer to Jesus, we must grow deeper in our understanding of both the definition and the origin of his love.

2. God's Love Is Perfect

This is a divine relief, especially for those who endure the exhaustion of imperfect love. We all do to some degree, but some of us endure it in ways few will ever experience. Those who go through abusive relationships, who are left by an adulterous spouse, or who are betrayed by what they thought was their most loyal friend endure drastically imperfect love. Yet God's love is perfect.

First John 4:18 says, "There is no fear in love. But perfect love drives out fear, because fear has to do with punishment. The one who fears is not made perfect in love." Two truths from this passage give you and me great reason to rejoice over the love of God. One truth is that his love is perfect. This means that his love is complete, mature, and needs nothing added to it. It is an absolute and final love. You could say, an eternal love. When all other loves fail, God's love never does. The second truth is that his love casts out fear. This refers to the judgment of God and the fear that we may have regarding his condemning us for our sins. Because of God's love, you don't have to fear judgment (1 John 4:16–17).

3. God's Love Is Made Known to Us through Christ

First John 4:9 says, "This is how God showed his love among us: He sent his one and only Son into the world that we might live through him." God's love is put on display in your life through Christ and through the life you now have in Christ. This means that God's love for you is not fully known by you getting your healing, because he also loves those who do not get healed. It means that God's love for you is not fully known by his giving you material things, because he also loves those who lack material things. It means that God's love for you is not fully known by your living the American dream, because he also loves those living in third-world slums. God's love is fully known through Christ. He is the common denominator for every believer. He is the reason why we can love others and say that we are family with those who have different last names, different skin color, different passports, and different languages. God's love to us being made known through Christ is a truth that changes your life and the lives of those you come into contact with, whether in a hospital bed, a nursing home, a high school, or a church.

4. Christ's Love Is an Example to Us

In John 13:34, Jesus told his disciples, "A new command I give you: Love one another. As I have loved you, so you must love one another." From that moment forward, history changed, because Jesus set the course for how love would change history. Love for each other would be a clear mark of a genuine Christian. Hate in the heart had to go (1 John 2:9–11). Even Christian confrontation had to be motivated by a desire to see people know Jesus and experience truth. Truth itself could never be compromised, but it would need to be spoken out of a motive of love (Eph. 4:15). The apostle Paul, who was known for telling it like it is, made it clear that the goal of his instruction was "love, which comes from a pure heart and a good conscience and a sincere faith" (1 Tim. 1:5). In Ephesians 5:1–2, Paul describes Jesus' love as an example to us: "Follow God's example, therefore, as dearly loved children and walk in the way of love, just as Christ loved us and gave himself up for us as a fragrant offering and sacrifice to God." This passage makes it abundantly clear that the Father is the initiator of love for us and modeled sacrificial love when he sent his Son, Jesus. Jesus is the example of obedient, sacrificial, selfless love.

Living Out Transformational Love

People who come into contact with the love of Jesus will be transformed. Like being hit by a linebacker on a football field, if you are struck with the love of Jesus, you will change direction! Nobody who experiences his genuine love can stay the same. You will feel it. You will be changed by it. That is Christian love.

So how should we be living out Christian love if we're to follow the example set by Jesus? As we go deeper into this chapter, I want to outline four truths that will shape the way you love others more like Jesus loves.

1. Christian Love Is Rooted in the Gospel

To experience or express the greatest and most fulfilling kind of love, you must first experience the transforming love of God. That happens when you believe the gospel, the good news that in spite of our brokenness, Jesus loves us and has paid the ultimate price so we can be restored and experience a loving relationship with our Father in heaven (2 Cor. 5:18). The gospel is what compels us to love, because the gospel is what shows us how unlovable we truly are. We may be cute when we're babies, but every adult knows that we grow up to be a bit of a handful. If you're a parent of toddlers, like I am, you realize that handful part much sooner! The bottom line is, from birth to death, in our cuteness and rudeness, in sickness and in health, we all need the gospel, and our love must be motivated by the gospel. This is an essential truth for you to grasp, because you are commanded to love and to do so in the ways I am outlining for you in this chapter. But like all of God's commands, this one is rooted in his grace, his free gift of love to you. This first and foundational point is why Christian love is based on facts, not feelings. Jesus saved you, loved you, and gave purpose to your life. His love for you is the starting point for your love for others.

2. Christian Love Is Others-Focused

In the earlier chapter "He Is Savior," we took a deep dive into Peter's words to struggling Christians about their need for Jesus to rescue their souls being even more important than their need for him to rescue them from trials. Peter commanded that group of struggling believers (to whom we can certainly relate in some ways) not just to believe in Jesus but to love each other like Jesus. In 1 Peter 1:22, he wrote that they had been set free and purified by the gospel so they would "have sincere love for each other" and "love one another deeply, from the heart." These words show us exactly who the object of our love should be—others. The word sincere means without playacting or faking it. Faking love is the very definition of hypocritical love. To be a Christian is to love (John 13:34–35). Just as God sent Jesus, he has sent each of us to the places we live, work, study, play, and worship (John 17:18), to be others-focused, to love for the good of all those we interact with. Do you love others this way? For all our differences in preferences, politics, and personality, do you strive to love others because Jesus loves you? Or is your love based on their doing things or saying things the way you like?

In 1848, R. C. Chapman, George Müller, John Nelson Darby, and Benjamin Wills Newton were intertwined in some serious pastoral disagreement. Each was a leader in his local church, so naturally their congregations took sides. In one instance, Darby's supporters wanted to make R. C. Chapman look bad and discredit him. They were more interested in winning the war than keeping the relationship. But it was Darby himself who reprimanded them, saying, "You leave that man alone; we talk of the heavenlies, but Robert Chapman lives in them." You see, R. C. Chapman had a nickname: "the apostle of love." Charles Spurgeon himself called Chapman "the saintliest man I ever knew." His reputation for loving others became so widely regarded that a letter from abroad addressed only to "R. C. Chapman, University of Love, England" was correctly delivered to him. He used to have missionaries stay at his home and required them to leave their dirty boots outside their door so he could clean them. That is love! Chapman could have easily behaved like a celebrity, raking in the accolades and wasting no time on trivial tasks like humbly serving others. He rubbed shoulders with world-changing contemporaries like Hudson Taylor, Charles Spurgeon, and the prime minister of England. But he knew the secret to life, and it was love. He loved others enough to serve them, to tell them the truth, and to live the truth he preached. Sounds a lot like Jesus' kind of love, doesn't it?[14]

3. Christian Love Is Unconditional

Besides the cross, there is perhaps no greater example of Christ's unconditional love than when he washed the disciples' feet (John 13:1–17). Judging by the events that took place that night, I believe this was the greatest act of love besides the cross. Why? Not because he washed Peter's feet. Peter was his imperfect but bold friend. Not because he washed John's feet. John was the disciple Jesus already loved. It was because he washed the feet of Judas. Judas was the backstabbing, betraying, conniving, thieving sellout of a so-called friend who turned Jesus over to his enemies just a short time later. He did all of this for a lousy thirty pieces of silver that he never even spent.

Imagine the unconditional love of Jesus as he took a knee to wash Judas's filthy feet. Think for a moment of the towel hanging from his waist, and his calloused but caring hands. Those hands took hold of Judas's feet, and while the Son of God could have crushed his betrayer right then and there, he began to wash. Slowly, diligently, lovingly, the Lord Jesus scrubbed the sinful feet that would run to aid in the spilling of his innocent blood. At that very moment, Jesus was the embodiment of his own words in Matthew 5:44: "I tell you, love your enemies and pray for those who persecute you." That he most certainly did. When we think about the way Jesus loved, it is enough to drive us to our knees, confessing, "I could never love that way!" But even though we can be such hard-hearted sinners, as we grow closer to Jesus and reflect on his love, he can turn us into tenderhearted lovers.

You may assume that by the phrase unconditional love I imply that you should let people walk all over you. This couldn't be farther from the truth. As our model for unconditional love, Jesus shows us that truth requires love, but also that love never compromises the truth. Warren Wiersbe rightfully said, "Truth without love is brutality, and love without truth is hypocrisy." Jesus doesn't ask us to sacrifice either one for the other. Look at the following examples of how he held unwaveringly to many key truths, yet through it all he was perfect and loving.

- Jesus tells a rich man the hard truth (Mark 10:17–27).
- Jesus unleashes sharp rebuke on the hypocritical Pharisees (Matthew 23).
- Jesus calls out Peter for acting like Satan (Matt. 16:21–23).
- Jesus reprimands Martha for not prioritizing what matters most (Luke 10:38–42).
- Jesus expresses righteous frustration with the disciples for lacking faith (Luke 9:37–42).
- Jesus calls false teachers wolves (Matt. 7:15).

Clearly, unconditional love does not mean compromising the truth. Nevertheless, the foundation of and motive behind every crusade for truth and quest for justice must be love. This is very different from what we see in our world today—and sadly, in the church. We may see people who claim to love others, but they are full of vengeance and violence. People who claim to love others, but don't tell them the truth. People who claim to love others, but take advantage of them to get rich. People who claim to love others, but are prejudiced. People who claim to love others, but won't talk to so-and-so in the church. People who claim to love others, but gossip and slander pastors and people. People who claim to love others, but stop supporting God's work or living out God's Word because of bitterness and offense. Is that you? Or is that *sometimes* you? It likely is all of us sometimes.

I want to challenge you to reject bitterness, push aside hatred, gossip, lies, slander, laziness, vengeance, cynicism, and lone ranger Christianity. Embrace love. Work at it. Pray for it. Choose it. Relish it. Seek to partner with others. Commit to careful words. Admit when you blow it. Respect others. Give love with lavish generosity. Be crazy about the church and those who need Jesus. Love what Jesus loves, the way he loves it. Not only is that one of the best ways to live out our faith, it is one of the best ways to prove our faith. Charles Spurgeon once said, "A loving spirit, kind, generous, forgiving, unselfish, seeking the good of others—this is one of the best proofs that our natural darkness has gone and that true spiritual light is within us."[15]

4. Christian Love Is Sacrificial

Let's go back one final time and finish our deeper look at the words about love from 1 Peter 1:22. Peter writes that we are to "love one another deeply, from the heart." The word deeply, which is also translated "fervently," has its roots in the idea of intense strain, feeling weight, pressure, being stretched. So the point here is simple: we are called to love one another in a way that stretches, pressures, and even strains us. Specifically, we are called to sacrificial love. Christian love is going to tip the scale of your life. You will feel it and see it. It will be both a blessed joy and a blessed burden. Sacrificial love is the root of true friendship and real marriage, and it is this kind of love that is genuine and Christian. Christian love will always cost us something. And this love must come from the heart. It's not forced or begrudging. This is love that *wants* to love or even *loves* to love. Christian love says, "I know the sacrifice it will take to love you, and I still really want to do it!"

If Jesus thought the cross was worth it to reconcile us with God, then how much more can we consider small earthly sacrifices worth it to enjoy relationship with one another? Can I lovingly ask you a hard question? What has Christian love cost you? If you have a difficult time answering that, I encourage you to look at three T's in your life: time, talent, and treasure.

Time is one of the most precious things in life. You can invest any given moment of time only once. You'll never get it back. Talent is your God-given ability. This is what makes you unique. Treasure is your money. It's a little easier to understand, because the concept is simple. You can invest it. You can make more of it. You can get something back from it. You can give it. The question in relation to Christian love then becomes, are you using your time, talent, and treasure for something that will outpace, outlast, and even outlive you? All three of these T's can be fervently, earnestly, and intensely focused either on you or on others. So again I ask, what has your Christian love cost you?

As you take inventory of those three stewardships that God has given you, decide today what action you will take to earnestly and sacrificially love others out of a pure, sincere, and joyful heart.

Putting Love into Action

For many of us, the natural response to this chapter might be, "Okay, I want to reflect Christ. I want to live out the definition of love I've read about and love like him. But what does that look like, practically speaking?" Thankfully, the Bible gives us a road map.

First Corinthians 13 begins by saying, "If I speak in the tongues of men or of angels, but do not have love, I am only a resounding gong or a clanging cymbal. If I have the gift of prophecy and can fathom all mysteries and all knowledge, and if I have a faith that can move mountains, but do not have love, I am nothing. If I give all I possess to the poor and give over my body to hardship that I may boast, but do not have love, I gain nothing" (vv. 1–3).

Then in verses 4–8 we are given a list of sixteen actions. These are not just cute sentiments to be read off at a wedding. These are a road map for putting love into action. This is what love does and doesn't do.

1. Love is patient.
2. Love is kind.
3. Love doesn't envy.
4. Love doesn't boast.
5. Love is not proud.
6. Love is not rude.
7. Love is not selfish.

8. Love is not angry or irritable.
9. Love is not resentful.
10. Love doesn't delight in evil.
11. Love rejoices with the truth.
12. Love protects.
13. Love trusts.
14. Love hopes.
15. Love perseveres.
16. Love never fails.

How's that for a great place to start? And if we're honest, we'll probably spend our entire lives starting and restarting, because the only way to walk out that kind of saintly love is to walk toward Christ as a sinner, over and over again. You are going to fail at living up to God's standard for love, but the more you spend time with Jesus, the more you will love like Jesus. Your heart is like a pitcher. It will pour out what it is filled up with. If you fill up your heart with Christ, you will love in a way that reflects who he is, and in turn have assurance that your faith, hope, and love are real.

Questions for Reflection

1. List a few truths from this chapter that encouraged and/or challenged you.
2. Out of all the actions listed from 1 Corinthians 13:4–8, which do you struggle with the most and why? Which are not as much of a struggle and why?
3. When speaking the hard truth to others, what should our approach be in both attitude and actions? Read

Ephesians 4:15, Colossians 4:5–6, and James 3:1–18 and add biblical truths to your answer.

4. How can a chapter like this strengthen us during hard times and draw us closer to Jesus?
5. Has the Holy Spirit convicted you regarding the definition of love and how you show love? Name one or two people in your life whom you can begin to love better according to what you've learned in this chapter.
6. List one or two ways in which you want to devote yourself more to Jesus.

CHAPTER 8

HE IS JUSTICE

"Listen to me, my people;
hear me, my nation:
Instruction will go out from me;
my justice will become a light to the nations.
My righteousness draws near speedily,
my salvation is on the way,
and my arm will bring justice to the nations.
The islands will look to me
and wait in hope for my arm."

—ISAIAH 51:4–5

In this chapter, I want us to go beyond the surface of today's debates about justice. Hatred and extremes can be found on all sides. As with every chapter up to this point, I want to steer your eyes heavenward. Together let's look to Jesus.

Turning our eyes heavenward includes seeing justice the way God does. Though this might surprise you, seeing justice the way God does includes hating what God hates. Some of us may think, "God doesn't hate! He only loves." But the Bible makes it clear that God hates several things, including pride, lying, slaughtering the innocent, false accusations, eagerness to do evil, dividing people against each other, planning to do wicked things, and injustice (Prov. 6:16–19; 11:1). God does have a righteous hatred toward these things. You should too. He also acts against what he hates. You should too. By mirroring God's righteous hate for wickedness and sin, you showcase his love of and desire for what is best for people. God wants his people "to act justly and to love mercy and to walk humbly" with him (Mic. 6:8). Sadly, we live in a world where the horrors of injustice leave us desiring a better world. We need a better way.

In his book *A World without Jews: The Nazi Imagination from Persecution to Genocide*, Alon Confino writes of the horrific injustices that Nazi Germany hurled upon Jews in their effort to ethnically cleanse the world of Jews and "purify Germany of the Jewish Spirit."[16] At that time, Jews across German cities were subject to countless injustices that included the following (and much more):

- In Berlin, Jewish physicians are excluded from the list of doctors approved to receive patients under welfare and health insurance plans.
- In Prussia, Jewish judges and lawyers working at courts are removed from office. It is mandated that the percentage of licensed Jewish lawyers should be equal to the percentage of Jews in the population, and Jewish lawyers are not allowed to represent the state.

- In Cologne, Jews cannot use the city's sports facilities.
- In Frankfurt, Jews must submit their passports for verification.
- In Bavaria, Jews cannot be admitted to medical school.
- In Baden, Yiddish cannot be spoken in the cattle markets.
- When sending a telegram by phone, it is prohibited to use Jewish spelling of names.
- The following organizations expel their Jewish members: German teachers associations, gymnastic and sports associations, the Association of German Blind Academics, the German Chess League, the Reich League of German Authors, and singing associations.
- The mention of Jewish holidays in official and business calendars is prohibited.
- Jewish businesses are prohibited from displaying Christian symbols at Christmas.[17]

That glimpse of history is enough to make anyone's blood boil. What's even more frustrating is that here in the US and across the world, people still experience mistreatment, injustice, persecution, and prejudice for reasons no human being ever should.

To say that the topic of justice is prevalent in our lives and in our world is nothing short of an understatement. It is not just prevalent, it is incessant. The daily newswire rings out with stories of injustice. People protest and riot with demands for justice. Undoubtedly, some politicians seek to exploit the great attention given to justice. And there is rage (understandably) over injustice. Debate roars on social media and in the streets, regarding

Black Lives Matter, the police, abortion, social justice, tribalism, civil rights, human rights, and religious freedoms. These debates spill over into the church at such an alarming rate that countless people are discouraged, hurt, or disillusioned.

We are a people in need of justice. But who do we look to for justice? How do we define justice? Who, ultimately, defines justice? And how is justice enacted?

If you ask a diverse group of individuals about justice and how it should be effected, there will inevitably be a range of answers. That's the challenge with justice and with people. It seems that many define justice on their own terms.

A story is told about a socialist who went to see the steel tycoon Andrew Carnegie. The socialist aired his grievances regarding justice and equality, and soon he was railing against the injustice of Carnegie's having so much money. In this socialist's view, wealth was meant to be distributed equally. In response Carnegie asked his secretary to make a tally of his assets and net worth, then divide his total wealth by the world population. Once the math was completed, Carnegie told his secretary, "Give this gentleman sixteen cents. That is his share of my wealth."

Like the clueless socialist, in the midst of our pain we rightfully cry out that life is not fair or that something isn't right. We may ask, "How could God let this happen to me? Why won't he do anything about this injustice? Why isn't my healing happening now? Why am I treated with prejudice because of my looks, net worth, or education? How is it fair that I am not afforded the same opportunities that others are? What should I do about injustice?" There is nothing wrong with asking these questions. I would even argue they are essential. However, we must ensure that the answers we offer, and conclusions reached, are sourced in Jesus and his definition of justice, not merely ours. It can be all too easy to let our emotions drive us. Jesus has called us to express our feelings and anxieties, but to put anxiety in its place (1 Peter 5:7) and lay aside anger, malice, bitterness, and slander, surrendering to him (Phil. 4:6–7; Eph. 4:31).

The Origin of Perfect Justice

Any Christian discussion about justice should include a proper understanding of where true justice originates. God is the very foundation and definition of justice. Scripture teaches that God's justice is tied to his righteousness. Because God is perfectly righteous, his justice is perfectly decreed. Anything that he says is justice, is. God requires perfect justice from all of his creation, and the Bible makes it clear that he will deal with injustice. It's never a matter of if with God's justice. It's only a matter of when.

One aspect of God's justice is his wrath. Some do not wish to acknowledge this side of God, but he is so just and righteous that he is even right to unleash his wrath to deal with injustice. This includes wrath toward the wicked who ignore truth (Rom. 1:18), toward those who harden their hearts in unrepentance (Rom. 2:5), and certainly toward the devil himself (Rev. 20:10).

God's wrath is just and right because "the wages of sin is death" (Rom. 6:23). God does not tolerate sin, because he is righteous. His ways are right and good, which means that his ways are best for us. Think about sin for a second. God hates sin. Why? Because he is righteous, yes. But sin destroys. Sin acts against God's will and his perfect creation and leads to death. Death is the antithesis of the life God created and called good. The court system must deal with lawbreaking by delivering painful consequences to those who hurt others, in order to prevent more harm. God must deal with sin in such a way that the chain of painful consequences will be broken. Only Jesus can break this dismal cycle. He is perfect. We are not. He can satisfy the justice of God. We cannot.

Just the other day I flipped through the New Testament and found more than one hundred references to God's wrath and judgment, *and* many references to the beautiful reality of being spared from his wrath and judgment because of Jesus. This truth should give us great joy, because if we believe in Christ and call God our Father, we can say without hesitation that we have the highest court and the holiest judge in all of the universe on our side. Better said, we get to be on *his* side.

We can rely on God's justice because of how trustworthy he is to keep his promises. Deuteronomy 7:9–10 is a strong reminder of God's character as a promise-keeping Father and judge of evil: "Know therefore that the LORD your God is God; he is the faithful God, keeping his covenant of love to a thousand generations of those who love him and keep his commandments. But those who hate him he will repay to their face by destruction; he will not be slow to repay to their face those who hate him."

A passage like this is a go-to because one of the greatest fears that we face as human beings is the fear of injustice. Few things cause as much angst as witnessing injustice. Whether it be a helpless child being harmed by an adult, someone being attacked because of the color of their skin, or someone innocent being charged with a crime, injustice can make us feel like everything in this world has gone horribly wrong.

In times like these, Jesus is who we must look to, the only one who can make things right. We can count on his being the ultimate judge. In John 5:22–27, we are told that Jesus has been given his authority to judge from the Father. Many people think that God the Father will be the judge of all things one day, but it's actually Jesus who will be. While the Trinity operates in perfect unison and each member is equally and fully God, it's a beautiful truth that Jesus is the judge.

Jesus, as the perfect judge, is (thankfully) impartial. He doesn't care if you're rich, poor, healthy, sick, black, white, Asian, Hispanic, Indian, European, Scandinavian, Australian, Canadian, Middle Eastern, educated, uneducated. He judges one thing: the heart. Romans 2:11 reminds us that "God does not show favoritism," and this includes the judgment that Jesus will execute one day. From the living to the dead, all who live and have ever lived will face the King of all kings and stand before his judgment seat and give an account for their life (2 Cor. 5:10). No one, not even monarchs and presidents, will be exempt from that moment. Every knee will bow and every tongue will confess that Jesus is Lord (Phil. 2:10–11).

Living Out a Jesus Kind of Justice

As with every other chapter in this book, this truth about Jesus is not just about information, it is about transformation. Knowing who Jesus is and what he is like shapes how you and I are to live. When it comes to justice, we do not need to give in to cultural definitions of the term or cringe with confusion while the news cycle broadcasts debate from all sides and people battle to gain our agreement. Jesus' justice is not about earthly politics; he is neither Democrat nor Republican. He is not bound to human parliaments or monarchies. He is the king of his own kingdom, ruler of the whole world. His justice is decreed from heaven, but it should emanate from our lives as his followers on earth. One day, when Jesus returns, there will be justice for all. No one will wander in fear, confusion, or injustice. The oppressed will be set free, the broken restored, and the wicked abolished. As the prophet Isaiah declares, "He will not judge by what he sees with his eyes, or decide by what he hears with his ears; but with righteousness he will judge the needy, with justice he will give decisions for the poor of the earth. He will strike the earth with the rod of his mouth; with the breath of his lips he will slay the wicked. Righteousness will be his belt and faithfulness the sash around his waist" (Isa. 11:3–5).

Right now the whole world is looking for justice. Yes, we need good justice systems, and we need to face horrible sins and call out abuses. So much of this has been politicized, but let's not allow that to derail our need to stand up against racism,[18] mistreatment of the poor, human trafficking, and abortion, among other societal ills. Still, our ultimate hope for justice must never be in ourselves. Vengeance does not belong to us. It belongs to God alone (Rom. 12:19). Our terms for justice, and our confidence in justice, must never come from our own power or biased judgments. Jesus is the final judge, and perfect justice will finally be done for all when the perfect judge returns. Let us long for that day (Rev. 22:20).

With the right definition and source of justice in mind, let's look at ten marks of biblical justice that every believer is called to live out.

1. Justice Requires a Deep Love for Our Neighbor

Hate is the farthest thing from true justice. Love of neighbor is the way of the Christian life and one of the practical ways we can seek the kind of justice that reflects Jesus. No matter how much we may think that our hate can be justified, it's just not possible. Hate is the mark of those who walk in darkness (1 John 2:9–11). Love is the mark of those who walk in light.

To illustrate how radical that love is, Jesus tells the famous story of the good Samaritan in response to an expert in the law who asks how he can attain eternal life.

> "What is written in the Law?" [Jesus] replied. "How do you read it?"
>
> [The expert in the law] answered, "'Love the Lord your God with all your heart and with all your soul and with all your strength and with all your mind'; and, 'Love your neighbor as yourself.'"
>
> "You have answered correctly," Jesus replied. "Do this and you will live."
>
> But he wanted to justify himself, so he asked Jesus, "And who is my neighbor?"
>
> In reply Jesus said: "A man was going down from Jerusalem to Jericho, when he was attacked by robbers. They stripped him of his clothes, beat him and went away, leaving him half dead. A priest happened to be going down the same road, and when he saw the man, he passed by on the other side. So too, a Levite, when he came to the place and saw him, passed by on the other side. But a Samaritan, as he traveled, came where the man was; and when he saw him, he took pity on him. He went to him and bandaged his wounds, pouring on oil and wine. Then he put the man on his own donkey, brought him to an inn and took care of him. The next day he took out two denarii and gave them to the innkeeper. 'Look

> after him,' he said, 'and when I return, I will reimburse you for any extra expense you may have.'
>
> "Which of these three do you think was a neighbor to the man who fell into the hands of robbers?"
>
> The expert in the law replied, "The one who had mercy on him."
>
> Jesus told him, "Go and do likewise."
>
> —LUKE 10:26–37

This story shocked the people who were listening, because in their minds everyone in the story was supposed to be loving except the Samaritan. If the Samaritan had hated the Jew, it wouldn't have been right, but no one at that time would have been surprised, because Jews and Samaritans hated each other. Yet the Samaritan's actions transcended those of the oh-so-spiritual priest and Levite. These religious leaders had plenty of legalism to offer the world around them, but little love. Jesus' story, and his command to love our neighbor, is a reminder that Christian love is not merely about telling your neighbor you love them, it's about showing them you do. This means taking note of their troubles, standing for justice, putting them above yourself, and caring for their needs. It means pointing them to Jesus as well.

You might ask, "Who is my neighbor?"

Of course everyone is your neighbor. May I press a bit harder than this for a moment? What if you considered that your neighbor was especially the one you despise or even subconsciously avoid? Take a minute and ask yourself who that might be. Someone on the other side of the political divide? Someone with a different skin color? Someone of another religion or social class?

That person is your neighbor. Now love them in both word and deed.

2. Justice Requires a Commitment to the Truth, and Righteous Anger

Jesus' justice is always rooted in truth and a righteous anger toward injustice. Jesus' justice is never rooted in lies or violence, and neither can our lives be if we are to seek out true justice. Do I mean that a country should never act with its military if a dictator is committing genocide? No. In describing this second mark of biblical justice, I am not drafting a treatise for pacifism or politics. Rather I aim to help us remember that we must never become the evil we are seeking to eradicate. While the world's system for expressing anger may involve evil acts like assaulting other people, Christians express their anger while maintaining righteousness. Some think it's permissible to fight injustice with harmful, illegal, unethical, or even violent means, like an extremist who thinks blowing up an abortion clinic is fighting the good fight, or protestors burning down their own city to make a point. Dear reader, this way of thinking is not in line with our Lord's. It is lunacy! Even Jesus, while he was here on earth, did not overthrow Rome for all of its wickedness. He fought darkness by overcoming it with light. He waged war on lies by proclaiming the truth. When he turned over the tables in the temple in an act of righteous anger, he didn't assault the high priest while he was at it. He aimed to clean out the corruption that had infiltrated his Father's house. He did not ever become the evil he was eradicating. Christians are to seek justice while never divorcing themselves from the truth and never resorting to sinful violence. In John 14:6, Jesus describes himself as truth and life, so can we live out his kind of justice by using lies and sinful violence? Of course not.

3. Justice Requires Patience in Suffering

You might be thinking, "How in the world is patience in suffering a mark of biblical justice?" You're asking a fair question, and here is the answer: while God does want us to seek out justice, he always wants us to learn patience while he administers justice his way. I call this the school of suffering or the school of waiting. God uses seasons of waiting to teach us, humble us, stir us, and use us. Whatever the process, the result is always his glory displayed in your life.

Martyrs who were killed for their faith cry out, "How long, Sovereign Lord, holy and true, until you judge the inhabitants of the earth and avenge our blood?" (Rev. 6:10). God's response is a calm and powerful directive to "wait a little longer" until his ultimate plan is complete (v. 11). What a powerful picture of how patience is a part of biblical justice! Are you waiting on God to avenge your pain? Rest in him. Jesus will bring justice soon enough.

4. Justice Requires Trust in the Gospel

If we truly believe that the gospel changes lives, then we must trust it to change the world. I'm not saying that we shouldn't be people of movement who take action against injustice. I'm simply saying that we shouldn't ever forget what it means to be people of the message. You can give someone a cup of water in Jesus' name, but if you've not given his saving message along with it, they may be more hydrated, but how will they be saved from hell? You and I should seek to meet their greatest physical need but never forget their greatest spiritual need. If you feed the hungry but leave out the Bread of Life, you've not given them food that will feed them for all eternity. Yes, do good works, but never—and I mean *never*—forget to preach the good news! The gospel is the power that changes lives (Rom. 1:16–17), shedding the old and making us completely new (2 Cor. 5:17).

5. Justice Requires Resistance to Apathy

This mark of biblical justice is a fitting follow-up to the last one because we all tend to think, "Well, I shared the gospel. I don't have to do anything else," or, "What is happening to those people is very sad. I hope someone does something about it." Have you ever experienced the joy of being that someone? No one can do it all, but we can all do something. Apathy is the antithesis of biblical justice. God is not apathetic to the cry of the broken, and we should not be either. So what are you doing to seek biblical justice in the world today? How is Jesus calling you to stand for his truth and to fight for what he lives for? Make no mistake about it, Jesus came to preach the gospel, but he cared about temporary needs and had compassion on those who needed him. Resist apathy at all costs!

6. Justice Requires Faith in Christ, the Coming King

Faith believes in what it cannot see. Faith is committed to something because of conviction. Faith is holding firm while others waver. Faith pleases God.

When it comes to justice, we must have faith in Christ, the coming king, and pray for the coming of his kingdom here on earth. As Jesus taught us, we pray, "Father, . . . your kingdom come, your will be done, on earth as it is in heaven" (Matt.

6:9–10). Rather than seek political power, we trust that as we follow Christ the king and seek his will, he will bring about justice in his own way and in his own timing.

When we understand true and biblical justice, we realize that we are battling spiritual forces: "Our struggle is not against flesh and blood, but against the rulers, against the authorities, against the powers of this dark world and against the spiritual forces of evil in the heavenly realms" (Eph. 6:12). Only Christ the king can defeat these hidden, malignant rulers.

In the meantime, however, we must have faith that Christ the king will be the ultimate victor, even when injustice prevails or "our side" loses. We must take the long view, knowing that "with the Lord a day is like a thousand years, and a thousand years are like a day" (2 Peter 3:8).

The author of Hebrews wrote, "Now faith is confidence in what we hope for and assurance about what we do not see. . . . Without faith it is impossible to please God, because anyone who comes to him must believe that he exists and that he rewards those who earnestly seek him" (Heb. 11:1, 6). Have you ever wondered why faith is so impressive to God? Why would this passage say you can't even please him without it? Because God knows that your rational mind naturally thinks religion is ridiculous. Spiritual concepts are foolish compared with rational and logical thinking. First Corinthians 1:18 says it this way: "The message of the cross is foolishness to those who are perishing, but to us who are being saved it is the power of God."

To be blunt, your knowledge isn't impressive to God. Your intelligence and reason aren't impressive to God. Even your Christian morals or commitment to noble causes aren't impressive to God. But trusting him when injustice abounds *is* impressive to God, because he knows you're walking by faith and not by sight. He knows that trusting in him goes against your nature. He wants your heart. Your surrender. Your worship. And living by faith is the ultimate expression of that. When you need justice and none can be found, put your faith in Christ and his kingdom. Ultimately he will make things right.

7. Justice Requires a Heart for the Poor

On this aspect of justice, one of the more convicting passages in the Old Testament is Proverbs 21:13. It says, "Whoever shuts their ears to the cry of the poor will also cry out and not be answered." I wish there were an asterisk and a footnote in which God added, "Unless you are sick, tired, busy, or chasing your own dreams." But there isn't.

John doubles down in the New Testament and goes straight for our hearts, declaring, "If anyone has material possessions and sees a brother or sister in need but has no pity on them, how can the love of God be in that person? Dear children, let us not love with words or speech but with actions and in truth" (1 John 3:17–18). That is pulling no punches.

God is telling us through his Word that our actions speak louder than our words. Biblical justice cannot merely talk love, it must walk love. To be followers of Christ and live out Jesus' kind of justice, we must have a heart for the poor, caring for their needs. Spend less time analyzing whether the homeless person on the corner is a phony and start focusing on how you can help them. Spend less time brushing off opportunities to help out at a rescue mission and join their cause to serve the poor.

Jim, a friend of mine, has been the president of the Orange County Rescue Mission in Tustin, California, for more than two decades. Under his leadership the OCRM has become one of the finest rescue missions in the country, serving the poor, the marginalized, war veterans, and abused women. He says it best when it comes to having a heart for the poor: "Serving the least, last, and lost is not about lending a hand out, it's about lending a hand up." I've always appreciated Jim's passion for serving the poor, because it is unapologetic and undeterred. People like him inspire me to remember those who need our support in their time of need. Our calling as Christians is to pursue biblical justice, and that includes having a heart for the poor.

8. Justice Requires Care for the Widow

Biblical justice also includes caring for widows. James 1:27 explains, "Religion that God our Father accepts as pure and faultless is this: to look after orphans and widows in their distress and to keep oneself from being polluted by the world." There is no getting around the fact that widows will be a part of our "resume of justice" if we're following Jesus. His care for widows was shown in a very personal way when on the cross he looked down on his mother, Mary, and John the disciple and said to her, "Woman, here is your son" (John 19:26) and to John, "Here is your mother" (v. 27). From that day on John took Mary into his own home. Presumably, Joseph was dead. Thus, even on the cross, with the weight of the world on his shoulders, Jesus' concern for a widow—his own mother, no less—was on display. Paul instructed Timothy to honor widows and establish care for them in the church (1 Tim. 5:3). Should we not also seek to love and care for widows? If we cross the time bridge from the days of Scripture to now, it's easy to apply our care of widows to the countless women in our churches who have been abandoned and abused. I also think of single women and women with special needs who need to be cared for. This sort of idea is often overlooked because we are quick to care about things that involve our own personal gain. However, if we are people of justice, we are to care even about aspects of justice that do not benefit our agenda. Psalm 68:5 calls God "a defender of widows." If he is described that way, we follow in his footsteps by protecting and caring for widows.

9. Justice Requires a Home for the Orphan

It is a heartbreaking truth in our world that faithful fathers are an endangered species. There are still some out there, but fatherlessness is an epidemic that shatters childhood health and well-being in the home. One study shows that growing up without a father negatively affects virtually every aspect of a child's life, and the impact continues into adulthood. Included in the long list of impacts compiled by researchers at Princeton University and the Harvard Kennedy School are that children who grow up without a father or a father figure are more likely to end up in poverty or in prison, and they are more likely to not finish high school or attend college. The study shows that nearly a quarter of American children under the age of eighteen live in a fatherless household.[19] That's not far off from twenty million children just in America who do not have a father caring for them. Extrapolate that to the world and you get the picture. Jesus cares about this. So should we. The Bible describes our God as "a father to the fatherless" (Ps. 68:5). This is clear evidence that God has a specific interest in caring for them.

I will never forget my first (real) visit to an orphanage after my conversion out of the prosperity gospel. I'd been outside of one, I'd talked about one, and I'd acted like I supported one, but it was all just for show. Orphan care in the world of the prosperity gospel was all just a show. Like a checkbox to make sure that donors were motivated to give more money (for private planes and Beverly Hills shopping sprees), orphans were a part of the money-making menu. But years later I found myself at an orphanage with a faithful ministry team, and the experience left me in tears, not wanting to leave. Within several minutes of our arrival, games began, soccer erupted, and the noise of children playing was music to our ears. Soon a young boy who was around four years old put up his hands, asking me to pick him up. A few others did the same to members of our team. We picked them up and within minutes they were fast asleep. One of the workers at the orphanage said this was common for the children there because of the constant stress the young ones were under. They rarely received the security and nurture of men and women holding them. When they did, they quickly relaxed and fell asleep.

Adoption, missions work, monetary support, and encouragement to others who would be excellent adoptive parents (if we cannot be) are all ways that we can care for orphans in their distress. I find it so interesting that James tells us to "visit orphans" (James 1:27 ESV). Of course, adoption is one of the greatest examples of what God the Father has done for us through Christ. Still, not everyone can adopt. But everyone can seek to visit, give, and encourage the support of orphans.

10. Justice Requires Defense of the Defenseless

Last but certainly not least, if we're going to grow closer to Jesus and follow him, we must understand that he is the defender of the defenseless. The Bible declares in Psalm 82:3–4, "Give justice to the weak and the fatherless; maintain the right of the afflicted and the destitute. Rescue the weak and the needy; deliver them from the hand of the wicked" (ESV). At the time those words were written, the psalmist was warning the judges in the land of God's judgment on them, and calling on them to stop presiding over the people with partiality and injustice. Instead God wanted them to be fair and righteous judges who would champion the cause of the oppressed.[20] In this modern era, we may not be under the same government system as Old Testament Israel, but the heart of God has not changed. God's perfect character is seen through his desire for proper treatment of those who are vulnerable and defenseless. Immediately I think of babies in danger of abortion; women and children who have been sexually abused, raped, and abandoned; refugees and immigrants; the poor and the marginalized; the physically and mentally ill or the special needs community; the elderly; the unjustly imprisoned; the bullied and the persecuted—all of them will see the great Defender come to their defense on the final day of judgment, and it will be hell for the wicked who have not repented of their sins and bowed in submission to him. But that should not stop us from defending the defenseless until Christ returns. We don't need to be healed to seek to help the abused and abandoned. We don't need to be high and mighty to help the lowly. We must simply step out in faith and obedience, seeking to live out the justice of Jesus as his hands and feet on earth.

Our seeking out justice the way the Bible teaches us to is a glimpse of glory to come. It's a shadow of the kingdom that the great King will soon usher into our midst. For now, we will never do justice perfectly, but knowing that Jesus will someday means we can trust him while we wait. In all of these things, no true and lasting justice can ever be found outside of Jesus. And remember, no matter how much we do to live out Jesus' justice in this world, humanity will not experience ultimate and final justice until he returns.

Questions for Reflection

1. List a few truths from this chapter that encouraged and/or challenged you.
2. There is a lot of controversy and debate over justice in our world. What are some of the wrong ways to go about seeking justice? Why do you think people opt for these approaches?
3. Why do you think some Christians shy away from the topic of social justice?
4. Even though the gospel is a message, when the gospel transforms people, it would seem reasonable to assume those people would live out their faith and change the world around them. How do you stay balanced in viewing the gospel as a message of repentance and faith while still being motivated to social action that loves neighbors and makes the world a better place?
5. Out of the ten marks of Jesus' kind of justice, which have you neglected or not thought of as much? Which do you live out in your life?

CHAPTER 9

HE IS SOVEREIGN

Then Job replied to the Lord:
"I know that you can do all things;
no purpose of yours can be thwarted."

—JOB 42:1-2

He is sovereign.

Those three words are like an iceberg, in that most of their mass lies beneath the surface. Many Christians will say they believe this truth, but few understand that we will spend much of our lives wrestling with it, whether we realize that or not.

When my son Timothy was diagnosed with cancer, this was the doctrinal truth that became the bedrock of our faith. Before that, we thought we had some grasp of it. But as you well know, there is nothing like suffering and trial to show us how little we truly know and understand. For us, it was looking at this chunky little baby and having to wrestle with the fact that God was in control and yet our dear son had cancer. If it is anything, the sovereignty of God is humbling for the human mind.

That God is sovereign means he is supreme and rules over all. There isn't a ray of sunshine, a raindrop, or a speck of sand that operates outside of his authority. Everything is under his power. If God is not sovereign, he is not God. The mere fact that God is sovereign requires that his ways be above our ways, his thoughts be above our thoughts. You and I are clay. He is the potter. He is the king, and we are his surrendered people.

That God is sovereign means you don't exist to do your will; you exist to do his will. The legendary Florida State football coach Bobby Bowden reiterated this truth when he was asked, "What's your legacy? Football? Your undefeated season?" He replied, "No. [Instead I ask], did I fulfill God's purpose for my life?" After forty-four years of coaching, multiple national championships, record-setting winning streaks, and a Hall of Fame career, *that* was his perspective. Such a strong and faithful mindset can come only from surrendering to what God's Word teaches on sovereignty.

Believing that God is in control even when things seem out of control can come off as crazy to many people in our world today, but if you say you're a Christian, you're called to think differently. A relationship with Jesus means a new way of living and thinking. The old is gone, the new has come (2 Cor. 5:17), and this includes your perspective. So while those who love the ways of the world focus on building their own empty kingdoms, you determine to build God's, so that in whatever you do, you do it for the glory of God. He is the sovereign ruler of your life.

A Heart-Stretching Story of God's Sovereignty

There once lived a man who was incredibly righteous and found great favor in the sight of God. He was a law-abiding citizen, a family man, and God had greatly blessed him.

One day the devil approached God, and God asked him, "Where have you been?" The devil answered, "Going around the world to analyze, scheme, and wreak havoc." Knowing full well the devil's game, God showed off the loyalty and devout faith of the righteous man he was so pleased with, saying, "Have you considered my servant Job, that there is none like him on the earth, a blameless and upright man, who fears God and turns away from evil?" (Job 1:8 ESV). With a disdainful quip, the devil dismissed Job's loyalty as nothing more than a transactional response to how much God had blessed him. He was certain that if God just for one second allowed anything challenging to happen in Job's life, Job would renounce his faith, stop trusting God, and curse him altogether.

In one of the most intriguing stories in the Bible, God gives permission to the devil to attack Job, stripping him of numerous blessings. Unbeknownst to Job, he had become part of a much bigger story line.

In one twenty-four-hour period, Job loses almost everything. First, he loses his livestock (a major source of income and survival), along with nearly all of his servants. But more devastating than anything, his children, all ten of them, are killed (Job 1:13–20). Upon hearing all of this terrible news from lone messengers who barely escaped the disasters, Job goes into great mourning. Even in the midst of his grief, however, his perspective remains clear. Instead of raging against God, he worships God, declaring, "The LORD gave and the LORD has taken away; may the name of the LORD be praised" (v. 21). Not once through all this did he sin.

But the devil wasn't done. He thought he knew Job's soft spot. If losing his wealth, servants, and children wasn't enough to break Job, the devil had one more blessing to take.

Another conversation between the devil and God unfolds. Again God points out Job, and he reminds Satan how faithful Job has been, even during his trials. The devil sneers, saying, "Skin for skin! . . . A man will give all he has for his own life. But now stretch out your hand and strike his flesh and bones, and he will surely curse you to your face" (Job 2:4–5). Surely anyone could endure losing everything else, Satan believes, but take away someone's health, and they'll trade in their faith for a healing. So God allows the devil to take away Job's health. Job is smitten with boils from head to toe and sits scraping his scabs as he mourns in ashes (vv. 7–8).

Then, as if all that were not enough—and anyone who is married knows that this one stings—his wife comes to him and instead of speaking encouragement into his life, declares, "Are you still maintaining your integrity? Curse God and die!" (v. 9). Job's response? "You are talking like a foolish woman. Shall we accept good from God, and not trouble?" (v. 10).

As we saw in an earlier chapter, several of Job's friends come to sit with him in his grief. For seven days and seven nights they sit in silence. Finally, Job cracks, cursing the day he was born (Job 3:1). And then the story takes a frightful turn. His friends begin to accuse him of doing something that made God mad, while Job protests his innocence. Job struggles with the horrible comforters his friends have become, and he begins to question God, wondering why God seems to be ignoring the injustice of his situation and remaining absent from his painful reality. After a long discourse from Job, mixed with praise, frustration, confusion, pain, and questioning, God speaks in a way that puts his sovereignty on display and puts Job in his place. "Then the LORD spoke to Job out of the storm. He said: 'Who is this that obscures my plans with words without knowledge? Brace yourself like a man; I will question you, and you shall answer me. Where were you when I laid the earth's foundation? Tell me, if you understand. Who marked off its dimensions? Surely you know!'" (Job 38:1–5).

Just reading those words is enough to invoke fear and trembling in my heart. Like you, at times I wonder what God is up to and cry out to him for answers, and like Job, we all tend to push back against God and make a case for why our situation is unfair. When it comes to the courtroom of our hearts, I don't know about you, but I can easily play lawyer, judge, and jury, declaring myself innocent on all counts and expecting God to see it my way and do things my way. If you think that's too sinful for a pastor to say, your pastor hasn't been telling you the whole story. Everyone wrestles with playing the sovereign over their own life and circumstances, putting God on the stand and questioning him to find guilt. Even Job, one of the most righteous persons to ever live, did that exact thing.

To that approach God says, "Will the one who contends with the Almighty correct him? Let him who accuses God answer him!" (Job 40:2). In response Job mutters, "I am unworthy—how can I reply to you? I put my hand over my mouth. I spoke once, but I have no answer—twice, but I will say no more" (vv. 4–5). Job essentially means, "Who am I to run my mouth at you, God? I'm nobody compared with you and have nothing more to say. I'm shutting my mouth and dare not mutter another word in my ignorance."

Out of this horrible trial, two beautiful story lines emerge. First, Job gains a renewed perspective. Shortly after God's roaring reprimand, Job says, "I know that you can do all things; no purpose of yours can be thwarted" (Job 42:2). He then answers God's original question. "You asked, 'Who is this that obscures my plans without knowledge?' Surely I spoke of things I did not understand, things too wonderful for me to know" (v. 3). He continues in humility and repentance, asking God to teach him.

Second, Job gains double for his trouble. Nothing could ever replace his first ten children, but God does bless him with ten more. Nothing could change the pain he endured, but God gives him 140 more years of life after this tragic season. From sheep and camels to oxen and donkeys, Job receives double of everything he's lost. He wears the scars of previous pain, but still God restores Job's life and blesses him so that he dies "an old man and full of years" (Job 42:17).

The lessons in the story of Job are many, but several truths emerge that are in sync with the rest of the Bible regarding God's sovereignty over all things and events. Like a deep-sea diver's oxygen tank, these are essential for surviving the depths of despair. God doesn't promise to remove all pain and make your life easy, but the Bible makes it clear that he will take you through your pain and make something beautiful out of it in the end.

Recognize the Truth of God's Sovereignty

1. God Is in Control When Things Are out of Control

If God is the one who defines good, and if God is the very definition of good, then we can safely trust that he has everything under control even if things are out of control. He knows the end from the beginning (Isa. 46:10), he owns the ultimate plan, and he is not incapable of handling your situation. You may not fully understand his timing or his ways, but you can find rest knowing that he is in control.

The book of Ezekiel is an outstanding reminder that God will make known to his people that he is the Lord, and as such he is in control. During one difficult season in my life, I was encouraged by a pastor friend to read Ezekiel. The book is quite long, but it's a fascinating read, and he assured me that it is a gold mine of inspiration. After a few more specifics, he mentioned that I should watch for (and highlight) all of the times when God says, "I am the LORD." Repeatedly God declares this truth regarding messages, judgments, and mighty works, to make sure Israel knew it. Over and over I found these statements, until I had highlighted fifty-six of them! Perhaps I missed one or two, but the point was made. Throughout all that Israel faced, they could be certain of one thing: he is the Lord, and he is in complete control of the past, the present, and the future.

God being sovereign means he is in control and gets the final word.

2. God Permits What He Hates to Accomplish What He Loves

One of the most well-known statements made by Joni Eareckson Tada, widely known for her life of suffering and her trust in the sovereignty of God through it all, is, "God permits what he hates to accomplish what he loves."[21] Since she has served the Lord for more than fifty years as a quadriplegic, those words explode with eternal perspective that you and I can learn much from. But she's a super Christian, right? She must be a theologian or have some special perspective on God. No. She's no more special than you or I, and she would hardly call herself a theologian, as she tells us herself.

> Ask my husband; I am no theologian. I've never read *Calvin's Institutes* all the way through, nor do I know Greek or Hebrew. But years ago, when I snapped my neck under the weight of a dive into shallow water, permanent and total paralysis smashed me up against the study of God.
>
> Up until then, I was content to wade ankle-deep in the things of God, but when a severed spinal cord left my body limp and useless, I was hoisted into a dark, bottomless ocean. In the wee, sleepless hours of my early injury, I wrestled against my Reformed upbringing—no longer were my questions academic, and this was no casual question-and-answer session in a living room Bible study. Lying in bed paralyzed, I fought off claustrophobia with hard-hitting questions. "Let me get this straight, God. When bad things happen, who's behind them, you or the devil? Are you permitting this or ordaining it? I'm still a young Christian; if you're so loving, why treat your children so mean?"
>
> That was over thirty-eight years ago. Not once in those years has God been mean. What's more, He has satisfied my questions with an intimacy, softness, and sweetness of fellowship with the Savior that I wouldn't trade for anything—not even walking. . . . When all these things happen, when famines and crib deaths occur, when snake bites and gas station robberies and pistol-whippings happen, God has not taken His hands off the wheel for a nanosecond. Psalm 103:19 is pithy and powerful: "His kingdom rules over all." He considers

> these awful—and often evil—things tragedies and He takes no delight in misery, but He is determined to steer them and use suffering for His own ends.[22]

3. God's Ways, Thoughts, Plans, and Purposes Are Higher Than Ours

A pastor once reminded me, "No matter what trials you face in life, remember that nothing enters your life that has not first passed through God's hands." While we cannot say with 100 percent certainty that everything happening to people is done by God, we can say with 100 percent certainty that everything happening to people is allowed by God. This can at first be confusing for our human minds, as we may think, "Why would such a loving Lord allow such painful experiences in my life?" We can't possibly know all the details and inner workings of his plans, nor grasp the full answer to that question until heaven. Isaiah 55:8 says, "'My thoughts are not your thoughts, neither are your ways my ways,' declares the LORD." When questioning why things are the way they are in your life, go back to this truth over and over again. Jesus, your Savior and Lord, is the commander in chief of the armies of heaven. Jesus, the one who knows your name and loves you with an everlasting love, can command every mountain to move, every storm to stop, the earth to quake, and sickness to flee. Why he does not do this the moment we ask, we will never know until glory. But what do we know? We know that our God has ways and thoughts that are above our own. When you think about how our minds think, that truth should cause us to cry out, "Thank you, Jesus!" Surrender is the safest place to be. Trust his ways. He is sovereign.

4. God Is Putting His Power on Display through Your Weakness

I can't help but think of the story of Ruth when I think of God's strength and power on display through human weakness. In the book of Ruth in the Old Testament, we meet a woman named Naomi who'd lost all she held dear. Her husband and sons were dead, and her daughters-in-law were Moabites. Typically, in those days, a woman who lost her husband needed to go back to her homeland. In such situations, it was normal back then for you to return to your native land and live where your people lived. Naomi expected this. She told both of her daughters-in-law that they had done enough to support her and that it was time for them to go back to their homes, families, and gods. She even urged them to go back (Ruth 1:6–13). But Ruth refused, saying, "Do not urge me to leave you or to return from following you. For where you go I will go, and where you lodge I will lodge. Your people shall be my people, and your God my God. Where you die I will die, and there will I be buried. May the LORD do so to me and more also if anything but death parts me from you" (vv. 16–17 ESV).

Because she would not leave Naomi's side, we are introduced to one of the most unlikely of pairings in the Bible—a Moabite woman who abandoned the rights, privileges, and care of her homeland to follow her Hebrew mother-in-law. Both were widows who in their poverty and weakness would have been fearful of their future. Naomi expressed the dire reality of their situation, lamenting to her family and friends that even her name (which meant "pleasantness") needed to change. She said, "Do not call me Naomi; call me Mara, for the Almighty has dealt very bitterly with me. I went away full, and the LORD has brought me back empty. Why call me Naomi, when the LORD has testified against me and the Almighty has brought calamity upon me?" (vv. 20–21 ESV). It looked as though they had been dealt a deadly hand and relegated to a life of purposeless pain. But the Author of heaven is sovereign over the story line. He gets to decide how the book of our lives ends and what purposes he will use to showcase his great power.

Looking back now, we can see how God used their weakness to display his power. God cared for them, God provided for them, God established them, and God gave Ruth a "kinsman redeemer," named Boaz, who rescued her from the desolate path she was on (Ruth 4:1–10). From the ashes of their devastating circumstances, Ruth went from being a pagan Moabite to becoming the wife of Boaz and the mother of Obed, who was the father of Jesse, who was the father of David, the king of Israel whose lineage led to Jesus Christ. Ruth, the broken yet loyal Moabite, found herself eleventh in the forty-one generations from Abraham to Jesus. And she became a legacy of God's power to turn any situation into something beautiful for his glory. He takes weaknesses and makes history.

Like Ruth, choose loyalty, obedience, and faithfulness no matter what struggles you face. Knowing what God can do, choose to see obstacles (whatever they may appear to be) as opportunities to bring God glory (1 Cor. 10:31), to embrace uncertainty, to trust him more and more. Choose to see your greatest challenges as your greatest catalysts for a deep prayer life, a firm dedication to obedience, and a fierce loyalty to Jesus.

Respond to the Truth of God's Sovereignty

It can be difficult to know what to pray or how to respond to the sovereignty of God. None of what I have written is saying, "God is sovereign, so you have no options. Do nothing, try nothing, pray nothing, and expect nothing." If anything, we must hold the truths about God's sovereignty in tension with our responsibility to pray, hope, trust, and act. The Bible teaches both. James 1:5 tells us to expect wisdom from God. Colossians 4:2 commands us to be devoted to prayer. Proverbs 3:5–6 tells us to trust in the Lord and not lean on our own understanding. No, the Bible does not teach passiveness, but it does teach us that we ought to have the right perspective on who is the ultimate authority over all the earth, and who holds our lives in the palm of his hand.

As we wind down together, I want to give you one final road map for prayer in light of the sovereignty of God. Over the course of this book, I have purposely mentioned prayer more than forty times. I want you to understand how important it is to what you do next. After these pages end, your journey with Jesus does not. Prayer must be your weapon. Prayer must be your power. Prayer must be your strength. Prayer must be your success. Prayer must be your life. As you seek him and rest in his sovereignty, my prayer for you is that these four responses will overflow from your heart.

1. Respond with Heartfelt Adoration

The sovereignty of God rightly understood does not invoke stoic intellectualism but rather heartfelt adoration of the Father, Son, and Holy Spirit. Some people come to understand a doctrinal truth like this and begin to think that because they have wrestled through a difficult truth or settled in on believing it, they are superior to others. They become obsessed with doctrinal rigidity but devoid of passionate praise. This is not the kind of worshipful response that God's sovereignty should trigger. Job had a greater grasp than any of us on such lofty truths, yet he remained a man filled with humility, adoration, gratitude, and praise. A right view of sovereignty means I suddenly become aware of God's position as the ruler over all things. The result? A posture of praise as I realize that the God of the universe has thought of me, saved me, loved me, sent his Son for me, and favored me. What grace! Can anything but praise, glory, and honor be the result? May our prayers echo the words of David when he praised God in front of his people.

> Praise be to you, LORD,
> the God of our father Israel,
> from everlasting to everlasting.
> Yours, LORD, is the greatness and the power
> and the glory and the majesty and the splendor,
> for everything in heaven and earth is yours.
> Yours, LORD, is the kingdom;
> you are exalted as head over all.
> Wealth and honor come from you;
> you are the ruler of all things.
> In your hands are strength and power
> to exalt and give strength to all.
> Now, our God, we give you thanks,
> and praise your glorious name.
>
> —1 CHRONICLES 29:10–13

2. Respond with Honest Confession

Is there anything more daunting while at the same time more freeing than open confession? Our flesh will whisper, "Don't admit the full truth. You'll lose credibility, you'll lose your reputation, you'll lose your power, you'll lose your pride." But if we embrace the truth about the sovereignty of God, we will find ourselves unloading the weights that so easily drag us down, and willingly placing them at Jesus' feet. Confession admits that I can hide nothing from a sovereign God. As Psalm 139:7 says, "Where can I go from your Spirit? Where can I flee from your presence?" What else is there to do once we've recognized that we can hide nothing from God? The heart and the head come together to express knowledge of deep needs. We need him to be our strength, because we can't do anything on our own. We need him to be our source of power, because we are powerless without him. We admit our total inability and confess that he is able.

3. Respond with Hopeful Thanksgiving

On a staff couples retreat after one of the most difficult years in our marriage and ministry, our pastor led us all through an exercise in hopeful thanksgiving. In one of the sessions, every couple was given a large piece of poster paper and was challenged to fill it with things to thank God for. At first I wondered what we could come up with. While other couples began to scribble down their blessings, I could think only of our burdens. After all we had been through that year, it seemed like we'd lost more than we'd gained, we'd been hurt more than we'd helped, and we'd had more conflict than comfort. But one by one the blessings of God came to mind, and we found that even our hardest circumstances had results we could be grateful for. More than that, it was the little things that started adding up, like food, shelter, and basic needs being met, then it grew to bigger things like friends, our church, our pastor, life, and our salvation. Sure, that was a tough year. But it wasn't long before we ran out of room on our paper.

Psalm 9:1 is a picture of hopeful thanksgiving: "I will give thanks to you, LORD, with all my heart; I will tell of all your wonderful deeds." Thanksgiving keeps us remembering all that God has done. When we recall what he's done, we become hopeful that he will do it again. A sovereign God is a God who is responsible for every good thing that comes into your life, but he's also not out to lunch during difficult times. Remember what Job said to his wife when she demanded that he curse God and die? "He replied, 'You are talking like a foolish woman. Shall we accept good from God, and not trouble?' In all this, Job did not sin in what he said" (Job 2:10). Complaining can come from many different things, but one of those things will be forgetfulness. Understanding that Jesus is more than a healer means understanding that he is deserving of your thanks no matter what you are facing. Whether or not the breakthrough comes, we accept both good from God and adversity—praying, rejoicing, and giving thanks in all circumstances (1 Thess. 5:16–18).

4. Respond with Humble Supplication

The word supplication means "to ask for something," doing so with an attitude of humility. This humility thing is a real theme when it comes to our response in light of God's sovereignty. Still, he is not some distant deity. His sovereignty does not separate him from our humble requests. We are to pray for what we desire, trusting his will no matter the results.

Several weeks before finishing this book, I was heading to a doctor's appointment with Timothy. His strong (but little) two-year-old strides next to mine, his favorite backpack on with toys and books in it, as we walked hand in hand into the building. His results were in from blood work and a bone scan. After we greeted the doctor, words came out of his mouth that were reason for thanksgiving. The doctor began by saying, "I am happy to tell you that his blood levels are perfect. This is what we've been hoping to see these last two years. I might even dare to use the word cured." He made a funny face and lowered his voice as he said that last line, the kind of face doctors make when they are happy but want to be careful not to overpromise something.

He continued. "We need to see this sort of consistency for a couple more years to be sure."

I replied, "We were originally told this was not something that would completely go away."

"Well," he said with a smile, "sometimes those little cells run their life cycle, and things just happen."

"In our house we call that a healing." The words just rolled off my tongue.

He nodded in cautious yet warm agreement, then tied off the checkup by saying, "Let's keep seeing these results for two more years or so. Also, no more treatments or bone scans at Phoenix Children's. I just need to see him every six months for blood work, then we'll spread the timelines out if things stay like they are."

You can imagine the tears of joy as I called my wife on the way home. We prayed and expressed our gratitude for the report, while also telling the Lord that we trust him with the future (certain or uncertain). Our attempt at humble supplication was asking that Jesus would continue to sustain what had been happening with Timothy's cancer, while at the same time doing our best to remember that his sovereign will transcends even the deepest desires for health and healing. The journey will continue, but our hope is that in all things, every trial draws us closer to Jesus.

Through the ups and downs of life, will we see answered prayer? Most definitely. But as the sovereign ruler of the universe, Jesus will determine what those answers will be. His being sovereign should draw us closer to him as we trust that if he is in control, he has all the answers, and if he has all the answers, he will know what is best.

If you take the first letter of the prayerful responses in this final section, you get the ACTS model of prayer, in which we spend time *adoring* God for who he is, *confessing* to God where we have failed, *thanking* God for what he has done, and *supplicating* God for what we need.

Our goal in growing closer to the Healer is not to gain the healing. Our goal in growing closer to Jesus is to have more of Jesus himself.

Closing Thoughts

It is my sincerest prayer that this book has challenged you, but more than anything, I hope and pray that these chapters have brought you closer to Jesus and renewed your mind in the midst of whatever you are going through. Whether right now or in the future, you will experience a time of testing, trial, sorrow, and pain. Never forget, Jesus is your healer. And never forget, he is so much more.

Questions for Reflection

1. List a few truths from this chapter that encouraged and/or challenged you.
2. Some people will use God's sovereignty as an excuse not

to pray. Even though God is sovereign, why should we still be eager to pray?

3. Do you ever get stuck in your prayer life? How might the ACTS model of prayer guide your prayers and sharpen your focus?
4. Having more knowledge about God can sometimes cause us to become puffed up with pride, thinking we are superior to others because we know more. What does 1 Corinthians 8:1 teach us about this dangerous attitude?
5. How has this book brought you closer to Jesus?

NOTES

1. You can read the full story in my previous book, *God, Greed, and the (Prosperity) Gospel: How Truth Overwhelms a Life Built on Lies* (Grand Rapids: Zondervan, 2019).
2. Nancy Guthrie, "Mother Faces God through Her Grief," interview by Cathy Lynn Grossman, *USA Today* (July 16, 2002). I highly commend Nancy Guthrie's work and ministry to you. Her books, videos, and small group material are a must-have for anyone enduring suffering or loss.
3. SuanlolZ, "Remembering James Montgomery Boice" (video), YouTube, June 15, 2020, 7:21, *https://www.youtube.com/watch?v=AOiio8N4WrA*.
4. *Alistair Begg: Knowing vs. Feeling in Worship*, Ligonier Ministries, August 7, 2013, video, *www.youtube.com/watch?v=KYNBdrFR5Bo*.
5. *10,000 Sermon Illustrations*, digital download, Galaxie Software (Biblical Studies, 2002).
6. Dustin Benge (@dustinbenge), Twitter, March 27, 2020, 10:03 a.m., *https://twitter.com/DustinBenge/status/1243584449851375617?s=20*.
7. Corrie ten Boom, *The Hiding Place* (Grand Rapids: Chosen, 2015), 171–72.
8. Donald McCullough, "The Pitfalls of Positive Thinking," *Christianity Today* (September 6, 1985), xx.
9. Matt Carter and Aaron Ivey, *Steal Away Home: Charles*

Spurgeon and Thomas Johnson, Unlikely Friends on the Passage to Freedom (Nashville: B&H, 2017), 96–98.

10. I encourage every reader to read the powerful story of Thomas Johnson in his autobiography, titled *Twenty-Eight Years a Slave* (originally published in 1909), and the book by Carter and Ivey, cited in the previous note, on how the lives of Johnson and Spurgeon powerfully intersected.
11. Mike Fabarez, "Forgetting God," Focal Point Ministries, accessed August 15, 2020, *https://focalpointministries.org/devotional/forgetting-god/*.
12. Philip Zimbardo, "The Age of Indifference," *Psychology Today* (August 30, 1980).
13. Randy Alcorn, "What Does Romans 8:28 Really Mean?" Eternal Perspective Ministries (March 21, 2010), *www.epm.org/resources/2010/Mar/21/romans-828-what-does-it-really-mean/*.
14. If you would like to read more about R. C. Chapman, I recommend *Agape Leadership: Lessons in Spiritual Leadership from the Life of R. C. Chapman* by Alexander Strauch and Robert L. Peterson.
15. Charles Spurgeon, *Spurgeon Commentary: 1 John*, ed. Elliot Ritzema, Spurgeon Commentary Series (Bellingham, WA: Lexham, 2014), 1 John 2:10.
16. Alon Confino, *A World without Jews: The Nazi Imagination from Persecution to Genocide* (New Haven: Yale Univ. Press, 2014), 50–51.
17. Ibid. This list is adapted from Confino's work, and more can be found at *www.facinghistory.org/holocaust-and-human-behavior/chapter-5/wave-discrimination*.
18. There are many, including this author, who prefer to also use the term "ethnic prejudice" when defining racism. I've stuck with "racism" here because it's still the most common way people describe hatred and mistreatment of people based on their skin color. Those who prefer the term "ethnic prejudice" seek to convey that humanity is one race, but people sin against

each other by being partial and prejudiced against different ethnicities. The goal of using "ethnic prejudice" is to help more of us see that we are one big family (human race), but we have unique ethnicities. It is sin to be prejudiced or treat unjustly those in our human family who look different than we do.

19. *Las Vegas Review-Journal*, "Help Cure the Epidemic That's Threatening 25 Percent of America's Children" (February 27, 2015), *www.reviewjournal.com/sponsor-old/help-cure-the-epidemic-thats-threatening-25-percent-of-americas-children/*.
20. Allen P. Ross, "Psalms," in *The Bible Knowledge Commentary: An Exposition of the Scriptures*, ed. J. F. Walvoord and R. B. Zuck, vol. 1 (Wheaton, IL: Victor, 1985), 854.
21. You can visit Joni Eareckson Tada's ministry at *www.joniandfriends.org*.
22. Joni Eareckson Tada, "Turning Evil on Its Head," *Tabletalk* (June 1, 2006), *www.tabletalkmagazine.com/article/2006/06/turning-evil-its-head/*.

ABOUT THE AUTHOR

In addition to being a pastor and author, Costi W. Hinn is the founder and president of For the Gospel. FTG is a Christian resource ministry that emphasizes sound doctrine for everyday people and features articles and videos from trusted contributors and Bible teachers. Costi is host of the *For the Gospel* podcast (subscribe/follow on Apple, Spotify, Google, and elsewhere), where he tackles important topics and interviews experts and influencers on relevant Christian themes. Visit *www.forthegospel.org*. To connect with Costi on Instagram, Twitter, and Facebook: @costiwhinn.

Printed in the USA
CPSIA information can be obtained
at www.ICGtesting.com
LVHW030420130724
785402LV00010B/118

9 780310 362869